HIGH WATER RISING

BY

Allen J. Smith, Sr

Author and Illustrator

Copyright © 2022 By. Allen J. Smith, Sr

All rights reserved. This book or any portion therefore may not be reproduced or used in any manner whatsoever without the express written permission of the publisher except for the use of brief quotations in a book review.

Printed in the United States of American

ISBN: 979-8-9862930-0-4

Email: smithajsr@yahoo.com

All Bible references are taken from the King James Version

Table of Contents

Dedications	1
Foreword	2
At Water's Edge	5
You Reap What You Sow!	21
Preachers: Lifeguards for the People!	24
Parental Obligations	30
Forecast For More Flooding	37
Water Rising in High Places	43
Nature Responds	49
Feeling Winter Fury	53
Coronavirus Pandemic of 2020!	55
Deaths of American Personalities	58
Economic Woes	59
Out of Control	66
War and Rumors	71
Prosperity - False Security	75

Danger:deep water! Turn around! Don't drown!....................... 80
Rescue 82
Where Do We Go from Here? 84

Dedications

This book is dedicated to my Lord and Savior , Jesus Christ.

I also dedicate this book to my wife Carolyn, my family, my church family , Pastors , especially the late Bishop Louis H. Jackson . Sr. , and ministers, and friends whose prayers helped me on this journey.

Special thanks to the team at Restart Enterprise who helped me publish my first book!

I Thank God for you.

Foreword

Water is the most essential element for life on earth. As such, it is vital to everything alive. Without water, life as we know it today would be non-existent. The benefits of water are innumerable. However, moving water can be quite destructive as its driving force changes the earth's surface. Destructive forces of water lead to erosion and weathering of the land over time. This brings me to the subject of this book, the global erosion of human values and respect, and the ensuing chaos that follows.

The horrible waves of crime sweeping through our cities are evidence of the surging torrents destroying generations of people. Waters once placid have become foaming rivers, bashing the foundations of this nation. At one time we were "one nation under God". Now we're so divided and full of hatred and fear. Hopes are being dashed, dreams go unfulfilled as the muddy waters of our sinful ways rise higher and higher. I warn all of us, the water is rising!

I was born in 1954 in Albany, a southwest Georgia city on the Flint River. Born the eldest child of strict Pentecostal parents, destiny would lead me from being a church boy to a church leader years later. My journey would take me from Albany to Augusta, and eventually to Atlanta. During this transition, religious training was the battle cry for my family. Church standards were adhered to religiously. I was reared in a family where dancing and attending the movies wasn't allowed. Television was even taboo and was often referred to as 'the devil with his tail in the wall'. The sixties were an era when families attended church together. Children said 'yes sir' and 'no ma'am' to adults. The wailing of sirens was infrequent, unlike the constant sounds today.

The moral climate of communities was more in sync with the biblical standards of the Bible. People were more concerned about being good neighbors and living peacefully together. Of course, people committed crimes then as they do today. However, the frequency and seriousness of the crimes today have increased greatly. The mindset of many people of today is much different now as current beliefs have changed. Sadly, much of what was once considered taboo is now accepted by society. People living in the 50's or 60's would be appalled at the behavior of today's society!

Many Americans, in our quest for a piece of the pie, have placed a higher priority on personal gain than seeking to become more Christian-like in our daily lives. As a result, God has been placed on the back burner. We've opened the door to increased depravity and evil that spreads like cancer among us. It's like venturing past the roped off safety zone at the beach. The farther out we swim, the higher the water rises on us.

One thing is certainly true, and that is Paul's prophetic statement (Galatians 6:7) that warns us that "whatsoever a man sows, that is what he shall also reap". It appears that humanity is obviously reaping the harvest of our misguided ways. God is the God of peace. Our world is torn asunder by divisiveness everywhere. Our children, who represent the next generation, struggle for survival in such a caustic environment. Their hopes for a happy and prosperous future look bleak.

When God first created this world, it was one of peace and tranquility. After Man's fall from grace, due to the disobedience of Adam and Eve in the Garden of Eden, the stigma of sin tainted the wonderful world which God had created. Through Adam's disobedience, human relationship with God became increasingly strained as people started the downward spiral of sin. Cain was the first murderer, killing his brother because of jealousy. Through the dispensations of time, man's ambition and greed led to more corruption and violence. Man could not direct his own steps in life, as acknowledged by the prophet Jeremiah (Jeremiah 10:23). Today, seeing humanity has created such chaos in the world, there is only one solution. We must turn back to God who created us to be spiritual beings. The Old Testament prophet Isaiah, admonished Israel to "seek the Lord while He may be found and call upon Him while He is near" (Isaiah 55:6). The wicked is asked to forsake his way and to return unto the Lord. Isaiah states also that our ways are not God's ways (Isaiah 55:8).

At Water's Edge

Years ago, our love toward God fostered deep respect for the laws of God, causing that love to govern our daily affairs. This formed the basis for the moral foundation upon which this country was founded. Over the years however, the sands began shifting and the waters tested our resolve to be guided by the principles of God. Changing attitudes and political correctness are drawing us closer to deeper water. God, in Isaiah (55: 8-9) tells us that his ways are not our ways, and as Heaven is higher than the earth, so are his ways higher than ours. Yet today we see obvious contempt for God's laws. People in general, make the choice to do what we want to do, regardless of what the Bible teaches. Need we wonder why the world is on a path to destruction? The rampant wickedness in our society spells doom and gloom. We have opened the floodgates of sin so wide, and the rushing waters of evil are pulling us underwater like a powerful tsunami! People, the water is rising!

While growing up in Albany, Georgia, my siblings and I did not have the option of staying home on Sundays while our parents went to church. It was an accepted rule that the entire family went to the house of God on the Lord's Day. I remember the many times that we'd be at church all day, especially on Pastoral Sundays. Sunday School took place in the morning, followed by morning service, with dinner afterwards. Then evening service would kick off and sometimes the people would shout until late night. It is the memories of those meetings around the 'pot-bellied' wood heaters and kerosene lamps with glass globes that proved to be my guiding force.

So much emphasis was placed on "staying out of Hell's fire" that one would be scared to do almost anything wrong. The consciousness of people was not as seared as is today's generation. People had a general respect for each other and as children we certainly revered our elders. The family was a cohesive and loving unit, resulting in safe and strong communities.

The early elementary school years in the Dougherty County School System helped prepare me for later challenges in life. To my teacher in first grade at Lincoln Heights Elementary, Mrs. Bell, and all the other teachers who impacted my life, I'm grateful. We moved several times while in Albany, causing me and my siblings to attend several schools. The first school I attended was Lincoln Heights Elementary. Next were Flintside Elementary, then Jackson Heights Elementary. I attended Carver Junior High briefly, and finally, River Road Junior High after we moved again. We experienced good times and bad and met many different people, but we learned to live with our challenges. Yes, there were days when we had little or no food. Besides being a holiness preacher, Dad was a cement finisher and sometimes the weather hampered his concrete pouring for construction. At times my parents struggled to pay bills and live comfortably. Through all our trials, our family still managed to go to church. People had their troubles, but the waters were not so turbulent then. Neighbors helped each other and watched out for each other's children. You could go to sleep with little fear of your house being broken into by thieves. Of course, there were spotted incidents of crime, but not in the magnitude of today's society. God was grooming me for his service that would occur years later. We were, in other words, 'learning how to swim'.

It was in December of 1967 that my spiritual awakening occurred. I and a few other young people had already been baptized in the name of Jesus. Days later, at the age of thirteen, on a cold December evening, I was filled with God's spirit, the Holy Ghost. As a teen I stood out from my peers because of my lifestyle. I refused to be a conformist. Like Moses (Hebrews 11: 24-25), I chose to suffer with the people of God than to 'enjoy the pleasures of sin for a season.'

I remember vividly the good ole days when we'd go to church Sunday morning for Sunday School, stay for morning service, before closing out the day with evening service.

Oh yes, I can see the old upright piano in the corner with keys missing, along with the big drum whose head was barely there. Of course, the scene is not complete without the wood-burning pot-bellied stove. The saints would shout all around that stove just praising the Lord! For seats, we had the old-fashioned schoolhouse desks of old. Lighting was provided by kerosene lamps. There were no indoor toilets. An outhouse at the edge of the yard sufficed. But oh, how God met us in that little church in the field! The church was our 'filling station' that gave us strength to go on.

In the fall of 1969, our family left Albany and moved to Augusta, Georgia to a little house on Walker Street. Sand Bar Ferry Junior High School was where my siblings and I attended school. By this time, I realized that my God-given talent was in art. It was my art that provided a safe escape from the 'worldly' vices. Bolstered by inner strength from frequent reading of the Bible, and strict boundaries set by my parents, I was not tempted to try alcohol or drugs. I purposed in my heart that I would stay in school and one day have a family of my own.

The formative years in Augusta were at times very trying for me. I was often the butt of jokes from fellow classmates who saw me as a misfit. You see, I kept to myself a lot, opting to be the 'good ole church boy'. I had committed my life to Christ and was determined to adhere to the teachings of the Bible.

From 1969 to 1972 I was a student at Lucy Laney High School. In the fall of 1972, I enrolled at Augusta College and worked through the college Work-Study Program at the Augusta Public Library. I graduated in 1976 with a degree in Art. After graduation, I moved to Atlanta to begin my career teaching art. These formative years in Augusta were at times very trying for me. I was often the butt of jokes from fellow classmates who saw me as a misfit. You see, I kept to myself a lot, opting to be the 'good ole church boy'. I along with a few other young people had already been baptized.

Even though I had many opportunities to do my thing, the indwelling Spirit of God was powerful enough to keep me from the temptations of drugs and an ungodly lifestyle. My father was very strict, sometimes too strict I feel, but at least he gave his children a foundation to build upon. In January 1986, my father passed away.

I moved to Atlanta in 1976 to start my teaching career at Crestwood High School. I could have tried alcohol and drugs, and whatever else I wanted to do. However, the calling of God was on me. As a youth, I had been warned of the vices of Satan and was determined to avoid eternity in Hell. I found myself looking for a small Holiness church here in Atlanta. After visiting a few churches, I found one on Capitol Avenue (later called Hank Aaron Drive) and I became a member of this Pentecostal church (also called Apostolic). It was here at the Atlanta Healing Temple Church that I began working as a Sunday School teacher and felt the call of God to begin my ministry.

Later, after several years of tutelage under the guidance of my pastor, the late Bishop Louis Jackson, I was ordained an Elder, later becoming one of his Assistant Pastors. It was in church that I met my wife Carolyn, who had moved to Atlanta from Chicago. She too, had been active in church at an early age. She loved God, having attended the Bethlehem Healing Temple in Chicago. We were married in 1980 and are the parents of five children. We were both very active in church and raised our children to reverence God as well. My pastor mentored me as I labored beside him in various ministries during revivals, conventions, Bible studies, and other roles. I am thankful that his teachings helped prepare me for the wave of evil today and pave the way for my role in church leadership. He was one of God's alert lifeguards who was more concerned about people's souls than their money.

I recalled one time when I accompanied my former pastor while he conducted a revival for a small church in Birmingham, Alabama. He wanted to do what he could to assist the pastor and the congregation. He ministered diligently that week out of a genuine care for the soul of the people. When the revival ended, the pastor handed him an envelope with an offering inside. I was not shocked to see him, without even knowing how much was in the envelope, graciously give it back to the pastor and say that he came to help the people. This was love in action!

Down through the years I observed the trend toward more relaxed morals and cultural decline in our society. As we study the word of God, if we're honest with ourselves, we will admit that as a whole, this nation has fallen away from the biblical standards that God ordained. Even after moving to the bustling city of Atlanta, I continued to seek God's guidance on how to be a true Christian. I had heard the Word of God since my youth and was afraid to venture too far from my earlier training.

After working alongside my Pastor Bishop Louis Jackson for some years, I lost my close friend and mentor when God called him home in November of 2016. Faithfully attending his Bible Classes, hearing his sermons, and getting advice from him prepared me for the crucial role that would ultimately become mine later. Those all-night prayers and fast days were a must! I now serve as a lifeguard, or minister of God. Following his death, I was installed as pastor of the church, Greater Atlanta Healing Temple Apostolic, located in East Point, Georgia, in December 2016. Now as a shepherd of God's flock, I'm really concerned with the direction that this country is headed in. I reflect over the past few years and can see the rising waters of sin swirling close by. I have been hired by God to be a lifeguard for his people. My duty is to warn all who listen that the water is rising fast, and we need to get to safety now!

Look all around us – in our communities, the entire nation, and even worldwide – there is a rising tide of trouble on every hand. Morale has ebbed, and the waves of discontent, corruption, and violence are dashing more with each passing day. Is this what "the home of the free and land of opportunity" promised? Can we afford to remain so complacent amid such turmoil? I am deeply disturbed by the growing trend of lawlessness and moral decline in our 'civilized' society. In the King James version of the Bible, the book of Psalms (9:17) states that "the wicked shall be turned into hell, and all the nations that forget God". Some may say that this is a lot of unnecessary babble. Be warned, however, that the water is rising, and America is drowning little by little. As it was in Noah's time (Luke 17: 26), people are doing the same things now. They continued in their ways until the flood came and destroyed them.

Most news is so disheartening now. Daily we are constantly bombarded with such disheartening news! One article after another report chilling accounts of needless murders and other despicable acts of crime. The senseless demise of civility and compassion has given way to heinous acts of terrorism, political corruption, and crime! It is a very troubling day when we can't even feel secure at our places of employment. It has become dangerous in the workplace, the schools, the churches, and just about everywhere! You aren't safe now in your own home!

Look at how far from the shores of civility we've gone. We see where groups of men feel it's okay to break into auto dealerships and steal several vehicles. Countless car-jackings, some with toddlers still inside, occur right before our eyes. Babies are being killed and dumped like trash! Surely, a nation that once took pride in its religious heritage, can't think that God is blind and does not see the evil among us! What was once deemed unthinkable now has become acceptable. That which was wrong is now okay!

There are some indications that point to the dangers we face as the water level rises. One sign of the times now is the appalling frequency of violence on school campuses. It is now reported that there were at least fifteen shootings at schools in the first two months of 2018 here in our country. Where did the breakdown occur?

Many of us look to our government for solutions to society's ills. Human government can only do so much. It takes more than more police recruits in the communities. Educational revamping is good, but has its limitations, too. Availability of counselors in school plays an important role in helping to steer our youth in positive directions. These are not enough! We must come to grips with the source of our problems, our own hearts. Until then, we can expect little relief from the surging waters around us. Divine intervention is needed badly!

These violent tendencies are only symptoms that show how deep the water we're in has become! Even in 1999 with the Columbine shootings, the message was that America needs to turn around and head back to the safety of God. We chose to ignore the warnings, and now we find ourselves in even deeper water. Years ago, around the sixties, schools practiced air raid drills to prepare us in case of attacks from outside enemies. Now we hold periodic intruder alert drills to safeguard students from attacks within our own walls!

The Sandy Hook Elementary School incident in December 2012 ended with over 25 deaths. Marshall County High School in Kentucky was disrupted with the shooting of at least twelve people, two of them homicides. More recently, in Parkland, Florida, at least 17 people died when a young man opened fire at school on Valentine's Day, February 2018. What's happening? These signs do not bode well for America. The farther we get from the confines of God's laws, the more turbulent the rising waters become! Yes, there are messages from the lifeguards (preachers)

that we need to turn back to God. However, it appears that more often than not, the messages fall on deaf ears.

Often the issues of gun control and availability of weapons spark debate. Some say that people owning guns is not the problem. Rather, the widespread decline in our moral values is the real problem! This decline is evidenced by disrespect for authority, for oneself, and for others. We've disregard religious teachings that reinforce good moral values.

Many believe that the problem is not that people own guns. It's the general decline in our moral values that's the real problem! We no longer show respect for ourselves or for others.

Society is showing disdain for religious teachings that guided our moral values.

March 24, 2018 was the day citizens all over America participated in 'March for our Lives' rallies, one of the largest cries ever for gun-control in our nation's capital! Some label it as one of the biggest youth protests since the Vietnam War. This discontent came on the heels of the February 2018 massacre at Marjory Stoneman Douglas High School in Parkland, Florida. Seventeen students were killed, and others injured in the shooting spree. The deaths of their classmates catapulted the students into action to convince lawmakers to address the issue of gun violence on our campuses. It was time to confront this issue of gun violence!

We're raising a generation that sees violence as the answer to their problems. Diplomacy has become a relic of days past when people talked about issues and resolved them peacefully. Have we forgotten the strategy utilized by one of the world's greatest peacemakers, Dr. Martin Luther King, Jr.? This drum major for justice preached non-violence even when his own life was in danger. Our society is full of people walking around with anger festering within. We have put aside God's principles that dictate how we live and treat each other. Hatred consumes so many of us. We see so much disrespect and contempt for that which is right because our actions show us what's in our hearts! Without God in our lives, the unregenerated heart is prone to do evil. The Bible tells us (Jeremiah 17: 9) that the 'heart is deceitful above all things, and desperately wicked'.

According to the Bible, ungodly lifestyles are summed up as the "lust of the flesh, lust of the eyes, and the pride of life" (I John 2:16). This is not the work of the Holy Ghost living within. Fleshly lusts lead to sexual crimes like rape, exploitation, pedophilia, just to name a few.

Lusts of the eyes give way to thefts, robbery, and other such crimes due to covetousness. The pride of life pushes one to seek success at any costs, often hurting others to obtain it.

Another horrific school shooting occurred in Sante Fe, Texas on May 18. Ten people lost their lives at the hands of a 17-year-old male student. Police reportedly found incendiary devices nearby as well. After the shooting, one student reportedly said that this type of incident was bound to eventually happen.

Why is school violence on the rise? Parents, as well as the students themselves, are deeply troubled by this alarming trend. Youth today are forced to cope with increasing pressure as our moral fabric continues to decay. Without divine intervention, an individual cannot face these challenges alone. Let us be reminded that Jesus said that without Him, we can do nothing (John 15:5). As a society, we've become so self-centered and rely on our own wisdom, and not that of God. How much quality time do we devote to God?

The 2017-2018 school year in metro Atlanta ended on a somber note for some. With year-end school celebrations just hours old, five teenagers were shot, four of them fatally. How tragic to celebrate our children's educational milestones one day, and plan funeral arrangements the next day. The lives of future greats snuffed out before they've had a chance to share with the world the gifts God gave to them. Will the tidewaters recede? It's up to each individual to do his or her part to help stem this menacing tide! Somehow, we must make our way back to God! Until we can see that we're about to drown, and turn back to God for direction, things will not get better. This generation is marked by much evil behavior. We must get back into church, not in a superficial way, but establish genuine relationships with God.

The violence continues. On October 27, 2018, another shooting took place in Pittsburg, Pennsylvania. This time it involves a house of worship, the Tree of Life Synagogue. Occurring during morning Shabbat, eleven persons lost their lives. November 7, 2018, twelve people were shot at the Borderline Bar and Grill in Thousand Oaks, California. The dead included college students enjoying a night of country music, along with a sheriff's sergeant. Then on Monday, November 19, a gunman shows up at Mercy Hospital and Medical Center, shooting a policeman and two hospital workers, before taking his own life. Allegedly, one of the victims had broken off an engagement with the shooter.

The rising waters of evil rose to a new level when another mass shooting occurred on Friday, March 15, 2019. In Christchurch, New Zealand, a 28-year-old Australian man allegedly opened fire on Moslem worshippers at two mosques during Friday prayers. In the aftermath, at least 50 people were dead with as many wounded also.

The riptides of evil just won't seem to subside! On Tuesday, May 7, 2019, eight students are shot and injured, and one was killed by teen suspects. This shooting took place at a STEM School in Highlands Ranch, Colorado.

Once more we see an example of how desensitized we've become as a nation. Our regard for the sanctity of human life is waning. Even though the perpetrator was said to be a licensed gun owner, the moral restraints were not present to stop him from committing this atrocity. Even the sacredness of a house of worship was disregarded! Why have the hearts of people become so hardened? God is love and people who don't love don't know God! (I John 4:8).

Just when it seems the waters are about to recede, we're once again inundated with more of the same. Another mass shooting occurred in Virginia Beach on Friday, May 31, 2019. A city employee opened fire in a public works building, killing eleven people before he himself was killed. Allegedly the gunman had emailed a two-week resignation notice due to personal reasons.

There is heated debate over gun control in our country. The proliferation of guns, I agree, does increase the potential for firearm violence. However, I truly believe the more serious issue to be the mindset of people with access to weapons. Until we,

God's created beings, allow our hearts to be controlled by His rules, the waters we're treading will continue to rise higher. This means that the longer we refuse to heed the warnings and turn back to God, the deeper into sin we sink.

As a society, we are paralyzed with fear seeing and hearing of the swath of death and destruction that sweeps our land. Just like Peter took his eyes off Jesus and began to sink (Matthew 14: 19-20), so we're sinking as well. Fear and torment lead to increased health issues. Medical costs have risen so much because we're trying to cope with these anxieties. The Bible (Luke 21:26), states that people suffer heart failure due to fear of the things happening on the earth now.

Still the treacherous waters show no signs of receding soon! Once more the murky waves of mass shootings continue to sweep throughout the country with devastating results. On the morning of Saturday, August 3, 2019, tragedy struck once more. Twenty people lost their lives while at least 24 others were injured. The shooting occurred in a Wal-Mart store in El Paso, Texas. The store was packed with back-to-school shoppers. The youngest victim is reported to be only two years old! All of this carnage happened at the hands of a 21-year-old man. A routine shopping trip turned into a horrendous nightmare for Texans and their fellow Americans.

In less than 24 hours, the demon of death reared its ugly head again. In the Oregon district of Dayton, Ohio, a 24-year-old man opened fire on revelers early Sunday, August 4, 2019. Before he was killed by officers, nine people lay dead, including the shooter's own sister.

On a smaller scale, but nonetheless just as serious, a gunman took the lives of three other people, before ending his own life in what has been termed a triple murder-suicide in DeKalb County, Georgia.

It appears now that the flood of mass shootings is rising! It is hard to predict where the next breach will occur. It's time now to rally the troops and join forces to stem the rising tide of evil that threatens to erode our very existence. When I refer to troops, I do not speak of the police and such authorities. They are doing what they can, and we thank them for their service. However, it's time for all GOD-FEARING people to resort to our weapon of power – PRAYER!

The answer to our escalating crises can be found in the Bible. (2 Chron. 7:14). "If my people, which are called by my name, shall humble themselves, and pray, and seek my face, and turn from their wicked ways, THEN will I hear from Heaven, will forgive their sins, and will HEAL THEIR LAND"!

My brothers and sisters, America is sick!!!! The state of America's spiritual health is not good. We see a myriad of symptoms all around us. The erosion of civility is unprecedented! Neighbors assault neighbors. Safety is a concern everywhere – Churches, schools, stores, even our own homes! Family members turn on each other more and more. Parents kill their own children, and vice versa, with little remorse. It looks as if we're losing our senses. In the midst of this spiritual battle, so many of our youth have given themselves over to Satan's vices. For so many, drug use has become a daily regimen. Never have we had to deal with issues like having our automobiles and other personal property taken from us at gun-point so frequently. Home invasions, smash- and -grab, sexual molestations, especially of children, are increasingly becoming daily news items.

GOD IS NOT PLEASED! In fact, he's angry with the wicked every day! (Psalms 7:11). The earth is deeply stained with the blood of so many victims. Their blood cries out to God to avenge their deaths. After Cain killed his brother Abel and thought he had gotten away, God told him that his brother's blood cried out to Him from the ground. (Gen: 4:10).

You Reap What You Sow!

Surely, we are reaping what we've sown. In his warning to the children of Israel, the prophet Hosea (Hosea 10; 12-13) admonishes the people to sow righteousness and reap mercy. During the troubles which plague us now, we certainly depend on the mercy of God to make it through each day. When one sows corn in the ground, he or she doesn't return later expecting to see tomatoes. What we harvest in our cities and towns are the results of the seeds that we have sown. The seeds that have been planted have sprung up and given this country a harvest of corruption, crime, and evil on an ever-increasing scale.

With our elected officials tumbling from their pedestals daily because of scandalous improprieties, and as educators and clergymen, and even parents betray our trust, it only shows that the sands of time are slowly shifting and we're slipping into deeper waters. America at one time stood on firm principles of doing what is right. Now we have treaded to deeper water where the footing slopes precipitously toward the dark abyss of unspeakable evil. It is time right now to heed the dire warnings and change the direction in which we're headed. Let's face it! We messed up! We need to turn back to God! We must do it for the sake of our children. The water is rising fast! I don't know about you, but I want the blessings of God upon me and my family. The Bible (Psalms 33:12) reads "blessed is the nation whose God is the Lord". I believe that as a nation we have pushed God to the side in pursuit of our own selfish agendas. Thus, we opened the gates that are releasing raging torrents of evil that we find unbelievable. Yet we do not change.

Jesus invites us to come unto him and he will give us rest (Matthew 11:28). It is not God's will for us to perish. Then why are so many deaths occurring among us? We have made bad choices. We choose to satisfy our carnal whims instead of seeking to see if our choices align with God's plans. The youth of today follow our lead. Where are we leading them? If the blind lead the blind, they both will fall into the ditch (Matthew 15:14).

Who would have imagined that American culture would be rife with such depravity and violence as we see now?! When did the dam begin breaking? Did anybody notice the cracks? Was there warning that trouble was brewing? Even now, are we still too blind to notice the water rising around us? There were warnings in Noah's day, but they went unheeded. When the rain began, people remembered the warnings, but then it was too late! The world today fails to heed God's warnings of the tragic consequences of disobeying God's word. The horn has sounded. It's time to get to higher ground now!

Allen J. Smith, Sr

Preachers: Lifeguards for the People!

Preachers are like lifeguards. A lifeguard is one employed at a beach or swimming facility to protect swimmers from drowning. They are responsible for the safety and rescue of people in water activities. They must be strong swimmers themselves to help others. They are trained to administer first aid as well. A lifeguard's duty is also to enforce rules to ensure safety in the water. Lifeguards must be focused observers while on duty and ready to intervene when danger presents itself. In the event of an accident, the lifeguard should be able to administer first aid to protect the injured. Also, a lifeguard helps to keep the area clean to ensure comfort and safety for the swimmers. So, the lifeguards, i.e., the preachers, are charged with the task of guarding society against the deceptive undertow of sin that is sweeping this land!

The church was once the center of life in the community. The teaching and preaching of the Bible provided the standard of conduct as we governed ourselves by God's Word. Alas, as time passed, we began to lay the Bible on the coffee table and relinquish our morals to carnal desire. Little by little human nature replaced our hunger and thirst for the spiritual. Sadly, entire families stopped attending church services, prayer meetings, and Bible Studies regularly. These have become passe. We are admonished to 'not forsake assembling ourselves together', (Hebrews 10:25), i.e., coming together to study God's word and worship. This verse lets us know that this is what some are doing now. Church attendance has decreased while crime has increased!

The abandonment of God in our daily lives has created many problems in our society-

drug epidemics, spiraling crime, a breakdown in the family unit, juvenile delinquency, and a general decay of civility we once proudly embraced.

This brings us to the crucial role of ministers in our churches today. God hired ministers to function as lifeguards for us. Unfortunately, too many ministers, pastors, and evangelists allow themselves to become distracted by the lusts of the flesh, i.e., greed, power, prestige, etc. God, in response to the wickedness of his children Israel, sent the prophet Isaiah to warn them of his

displeasure with them. In the book of Isaiah (58:1), Isaiah was told to 'cry aloud, spare not, lift up his voice like a trumpet, and show my people their transgression, and the house of Jacob their sins'. Just as lifeguards must be watchful and warn those in the water of imminent danger, the minister has a charge from God to warn society of impending danger. The waters all around us are turbulent and closing in on us. God's lifeguards must not hesitate to blow the whistles to warn the people of the impending dangers lurking beneath the waters. Yet we frolic without care, oblivious of the current that is pulling us into deep water.

As a retired middle school educator, I've seen the detriment that now drowns our youth with wave after wave of despair and hopelessness. Drugs, gangs, sexploitation of children, political corruption, poverty, just to name a few, are some forces that create the riptides that push this nation further away from the safety of God. In the search for the 'good life', too often we fail to adhere to Godly principles, that is to love God first, and our neighbors as ourselves. America is swimming in troubled waters. It is the duty of God's lifeguards, the ministers, to warn the people of the danger of leaving the safety of God's laws and love.

The sea of humanity is raging partly because of the incompetence of those who profess to be our rescuers. It is a sad day when these spiritual lifeguards prey on the victims they've been called to save. Sexual predators, even among clergy and educators, has contributed to a growing wave of distrust. Where are the godly leaders? Where are the praying Christians?

First, our civic and ecclesiastical leaders must themselves exemplify high moral standards if they are to positively affect the populace. The Bible states that if the blind lead the blind, both of them will fall into the ditch (Matthew 15:14). Too often leaders in church, education, and government have betrayed our trust by giving in to ungodly vices. Respect for leadership is undermined when this happens. This opens the door to lawlessness, especially to our youth. Floodwaters around us now teem with the pollution of evil!

In the Old Testament, God sent the prophet Jeremiah to deliver a message especially to the pastors. In the warning (Jeremiah 23:1) God pronounced doom upon the pastors that destroy and scatter the sheep, meaning his people. Today the message is still just as strong as it was then. Countless pastors have caused their congregations to lose faith in the Church because of the sinful behaviors of the spiritual leaders who should be leading by example.

In February 2018, America lost one of its greatest preachers, Reverend Billy Graham, who passed away at the age of 99. This spiritual lifeguard's ministry spanned the

offices of about twelve American presidents. His goal was not to be flamboyant, but to present the Gospel to all so that God received the glory, and not himself. For years he warned America and millions of others in his campaigns and telecasts to flee the rising waters of sin. His concern for the souls of men and women will stand as testimony against many in the Judgement. Unlike many of today's ministers, he conducted himself in a manner so as not to bring reproach upon the ministry. He tried to warn the people of the approaching tsunami of evil.

In the fourth chapter of the book of Hosea in the Bible (Hosea 4:6) God states that his people are destroyed due to the 'lack of knowledge'. God has a controversy with the inhabitants of the land because 'there is no truth, nor mercy, nor knowledge of God in the land'. We have become a nation of pleasure seekers with little or no time for God. People simply do what pleases them and disregard God's laws, giving little thought to the consequences.

When I see and read the news I wonder if people realize how angry God is because of our behaviors. It is true that God is love and it is not His will for anyone to perish but have eternal life (John

3:16). However, the scriptures also let us know that 'God is angry with the wicked 'every day' (Psalms 7: 11). Many of the things that we've come to accept as a way of life are evil abominations in God's view. Political correctness supersedes the righteousness of God's law in our society. We've allowed ourselves to get into deep water and the preachers are afraid to warn us. The quest for huge cathedrals and large congregations feeds the tills of greediness and have distracted many, not all, preachers from telling us the truth. God hired the preachers to go into the vineyards and work as 'watchmen on the wall'. Preachers are the watchmen (Ezekiel 3:17) and have a commandment from God to warn the wicked. If the wicked die because the preacher did not warn him, God says that his blood will be 'required at the preacher's hand'. However, if the preacher warns the people of their sin and they refuse to repent, they shall die, but the preacher has delivered himself because he spoke God's word.

Presently, the world is in chaos, and it is because we choose to follow the wrong paths. When humans blatantly disregard the laws that God ordained for the human family to abide by, we open the gates to the floodwaters of evil that pervade our society now. As a result, we are experiencing anguish and sorrow beyond comprehension. The cause of so many of our troubles can be found in the Bible.

God, in his Word (Proverbs 1:24-31) tells us He has called, but we refuse to hear. We don't want Him to correct us, and we hate knowledge of Him. As a result, he will mock us when our fears are upon us! Parents kill their own offspring and exhibit no remorse. Murderers increasingly snuff out the lives of innocent people, with all types of crimes escalating in our cities. It seems that the more money and resources that are allocated to deter criminals, the more havoc they wreak.

God's word in the book of Isaiah (26:9) says that "when God's judgements are in the earth, the inhabitants of the world will learn righteousness". We refuse to accept the fact that God is angry because of the lifestyles that we have chosen. The sexual mores of today have replaced God's code of conduct by condoning such depravity as exists in our streets today. Despite its acceptance by society, homosexuality was condemned by God from days of old (Leviticus 18:22) and is an abomination in God's sight. It is mind-boggling to even think of the horrendous sexual abuse of children today! Large cities like Atlanta have become trading centers for such wicked vices, destroying the futures for so many innocent young people. Where are the lifeguards, i.e., the preachers who are to rescue them from such strong undercurrents in our land? The lifeguards must stay on their posts, peering out over the ocean of humanity, and caution the people that we are getting in water over our heads.

Of many preachers, God characterize them as 'blind watchmen, dumb dogs that cannot bark, greedy and can never get enough, working for his own gain' (Isaiah 56: 10 -11). This simply means that the preachers must no longer be silent on these issues but speak out against all evil practices that contradict God's word so that America can be great again! The Apostle Paul in one of his letters to Timothy (2 Timothy 4: 1- 4), admonishes Timothy to preach the Word, because the time will come when people won't want to hear sound doctrine. That time is now!

Parental Obligations

Children once were respectful not only to their parents, but to adults in general. As primary caretakers of children, parents nurtured, loved, and wanted the best for our children. We tried to shield them from evil and wanted to ensure that they had opportunities to grow into happy, healthy, and productive citizens. Thanks to those parents who still believe in the principle that 'you reap what you sow'. Education and good work ethics guided by godly principles for living produce great results.

Too many parents now leave their children in the care of electronic babysitters, i.e., television and computer games to entertain them and keep them occupied. I often think of the boredom for youth if a power failure were to happen for a period. We are so into our cell phones and electronic gadgets that we've lost touch with good communication skills.

Looking at the erosive behavior of the youth today (I speak in general terms here), it is obvious to me that they are not familiar with the biblical warnings from God as stated in the Bible (Ecclesiastes 11:9-10). It seems that people feel they have a license to kill, steal, and destroy people and property

It is mind-boggling to think about the atrocities that are committed by humans who feel justified in doing them! It is common news to hear of senior citizens preyed upon, their property taken, and even losing their lives so unnecessarily. Thieves wait for packages to be delivered to homes, only to run onto porches and snatch someone else's property. Others break into businesses and homes stealing valuables, automobiles. People, the water is rising around us and it doesn't look good! The Apostle Peter admonished those listening to him on the Day of Pentecost to save themselves from this untoward generation (Acts 2: 40). Truly this is a very wicked time in the history of mankind!

Young people need to know that disrespect for one's parents is a direct violation of God's commandment with a promise (Ephesians 6:2, Exodus 20:12). Children are admonished to honor their fathers and mothers. The benefit of doing so is to live long and have things go well in their lives.

Too many of our youth are dying sooner than they should simply because they refuse to accept advice and wisdom from parents and other adults who've already travelled the paths that they are trying to navigate. There are some very responsible youths among us today. I am grateful to God that all respect has not disappeared from society. Unfortunately, though, there are some who want the finer things of life, but patience is not one of their virtues. The tried-and-true work ethic does not appeal to them. They want what they want right now! A lot of people expect great gain with the least amount of effort on their part. Apostle

Paul stated that if any would not work, neither should he eat (2 Thess. 3:10).

Social media has its role in our modern society. Unfortunately, it has also opened another spigot of evil that trickles down to our young people today. Pornography has become big business. Our young children are being robbed of childhood innocence by ruthless sexual predators who promise an escape from loneliness and poverty. Instead, the children fall prey to the sadistic desires of those who should be their protectors.

Today the lack of discipline is evident in our culture everywhere we turn. Being raised by two God-fearing parents, I learned early that being a child meant limitations on what I could do and speak. As a classroom teacher, the challenges were many. This generation of young people uses more profanity than ever, even to parents. This is not entirely the children's fault! As adults, the parents must be held to blame. As a son, I cannot recall ever hearing my parents curse or call people unthinkable names as people do now. The book of Ephesians 6:1- 3 says children are to honor their parents. It goes on to say that if children did this, things would be well for them, and that they would live a long life. Wow! The question is then why are so many of our youth dying so young? Yes. They are rebellious at the world that we have created for them. Adults speak one thing but do another. The examples we show them glorify cheating, sexual promiscuity, dishonesty, and other lifestyles that drag society under water. The water is rising and rising fast! Are we to just see the approaching water and make no move to save ourselves?

We live with too much hatred among us! The senseless murders of innocent people and gross miscarriage of justice should serve as a wake-up call to America. Obviously, we're headed in the wrong direction. Jesus pleads with us to look unto

Him, all ends of the earth, and be saved! We tread thoughtlessly on God's principles for righteous living, seemingly oblivious to the consequences to follow.

Parents used to take their children to church, exposing them to biblical principles to help mold character that developed them into respectable citizens who contributed value to the community. Now so many people don't have time for God, and our children take their cue from us. Our neighborhoods are becoming prisons of fear and distrust as neighbor preys upon neighbor, parent against child, child against parent, and utter disdain for the right. Things would be much better for all if we as parents heeded God's directive to "train up a child in the way he should go so that when he is old,he will not depart from it". (Proverbs 22:6). What caring parent stands quietly on the beach watching a towering wave of water rush toward their young child about to be washed away?! This is what we're allowing to happen to our youth. Good examples start at home first. Adults, let's look at our own behaviors. What examples are we to the youth today? Are we role models that exemplify good character? Children watch us fight, steal, curse, commit adultery, and so many other evil things. They imitate what they see! Unfortunately, too many adults are not showing the youth much good character.

Look at the heinous acts of wickedness that casts a dreadful pall over the land today. In January 2018, a California couple was arrested for gross child abuse of their thirteen children over several years. This horrific case sent shock waves around the world. Parents, who were supposed to raise and nurture their offspring, instead starved and chained them to beds in squalid condition amid filth. Not until one of them escaped and sought help was their plight discovered. The Apostle Paul urged parents to not provoke their children to wrath (Ephesians 6:4) but bring them up in the nurture and admonition of the Lord.

Back in January 2018 in Kentucky, two students were killed and at least 16 others injured when a student opened fire at Marshall County High School. Just another sign of the restlessness in society that has evolved as this country wades into deeper water. The book of Hebrews (Hebrews 12:14) advises us to follow peace with all men, and holiness, without which no man shall see the Lord.

Even the entertainment industry affects how society is today. Song lyrics and movies that once expressed sentiments of love and respect and motivated people to think of wholesome lifestyles have given way to words and images that defy authority, encourage violence, and glorify negative behaviors. We are commanded (Ephesians 4:29) to not allow corrupt communication come out of our mouth. Yet we hear profanities and vulgar language spoken in front of even toddlers. This is one reason today's youth act the way they do, because adults' behavior gives them such license. Elementary school children have already been exposed to so much violence in the neighborhood and in the media before they even get to middle school.

In January 2019 I returned to the classroom as a substitute teacher, working with elementary grades. It's disheartening to see even the young kids so angry and violent so early in their lives So many are not accustomed to a "Good Morning" as they enter the classroom. It's as if they do not expect people to treat them with kindness and respect. Good manners appear to be relics of the past.

I've conversed with too many perplexed educators who prepared themselves to help our youth become informed and productive citizens of the future. Many now feel that the countless hours of study and untold thousands of dollars spent in institutions of higher learning to become educators did not equip us to fully deal with the problems in academia today.

A key issue in schools today is discipline. There is general agreement on this subject among educators nationwide. I certainly understand the plight of teachers who are passionate about equipping students with knowledge and wisdom to be productive citizens. It is hurtful when a student asks a teacher for permission to go 'to another classroom' when disruptive students hinder their ability to learn.

Yes, there is a huge breakdown in discipline training in the home! Even the young elementary students used profanity regularly. Children are yelled at, cursed, and mistreated at home. This is what they hear and see daily, and they bring all this baggage to the classroom.

Their interaction with those around them is based on what they see at home.

Times have changed understandably. However, some things in the past were helpful. As a boy I often recall the 'Blue Laws' in Georgia. Such laws were originally designed to enforce religious standards. Late Saturday evening, many businesses closed until the next week, recognizing Sunday as the Lord's Day, a time for families to honor God. Today those laws are only memories as capitalism and the pursuit of happiness have come to the forefront. Parents must do their part to help rescue our world from the coming wave of destruction! The water is rising fast! Help us save the children!

Forecast For More Flooding

I don't want to be the bearer of bad news. The meteorologist giving the weather report would love to predict beautiful sunny skies instead of a looming thunderstorm. When I read God's Word, the forecast bodes for ill winds and flood conditions. The Apostle Paul, in his epistle (2 Timothy, Chapter 3) to the young Pastor Timothy, warns him that perilous times are ahead. Even today, the forecast is dire! We are in danger of some serious harm brought on by the fold of evil in this country. Apostle Paul enumerates the conditions that precede the advancing floodwaters. He describes indicators such as people who are unthankful, disobedient to parents, false accusers, despisers of those who are good, and those who love pleasure more than they love God. These are just some of the ripples that soon become a major flood.

In verse 13 of the same book, our hopes for a better forecast are dashed when the apostle states that 'evil men shall wax worse and worse". That is not very comforting, but we can avert disaster by heeding the warning signs around us and returning to God as a nation! We hear and see the menacing waves of destruction swirling through our communities daily.

High Water Rising

The first human murder occurred when a jealous Cain killed his brother Abel (Genesis 4:8). The Lord told Cain that his brother's blood cried to Him from the ground. Wow! Can you imagine today the blood of multitudes of people crying out to God? God's commandment that forbids the taking of another human's life has been set aside. Murders have now become commonplace in our society.

Parents and their children are killing each other at an alarming rate. Once upon a time it was safe to go just about anywhere at any time. Now even home is not the haven it used to be. Our planet earth must certainly be moaning as it becomes saturated with the blood of so many people!

Still the treacherous waters show no sign of receding soon! Once more the murky waves of mass shootings continue to sweep through our country. On Saturday morning, August 3, 2019, twenty people lost their lives, with at least twenty-four others being wounded. The shooting occurred in a Wal-Mart store in El Paso, Texas. The store was packed with back-to-school shoppers. The youngest victim was said to be only two years old! All of this carnage took place at the hands of a 21-year-old man. A routine shopping trip turned into a horrendous nightmare for Texans and fellow Americans.

In less than twenty-four hours, the demon of death reared its ugly head again. Early Sunday

morning, August 4, the suspected shooter, a twenty-four-year-old man, opened fire on revelers in the Oregon district of Dayton, Ohio. Before he was killed by officers, nine people lay dead, including the shooter's own sister.

On a smaller scale, but nonetheless just as serious, a gunman took the lives of three persons before ending his own in a triple murder-suicide. This happened Tuesday, August 6, in DeKalb County, Georgia. So, we see, the blood-stained waters of murder rise higher around us! It is hard to predict where the next breach will occur.

It is time to assemble the troops and join forces to stem the rising tide of evil that threatens to erode our very existence. When I refer to troops, I'm not speaking of civil authorities only. It is time for all God-fearing people to resort to our weapon of defense – PRAYER!

The answer to America's woes can be found in our safety manual – the BIBLE! God who is our help says "If my people, which are called by my name, shall humble themselves, and pray, and seek my face, and turn from their wicked ways, THEN will I hear from Heaven, will forgive their sin, and will HEAL THEIR LAND". (2 Chron. 7:14).

There are many good-hearted youths among us today. Unfortunately, the rising waters of ungodliness is taking a terrible toll on our young generation. Never have we heard of so many home invasions, car thefts, robberies, and shootings as we do in this day and time. Of course, there is a reason for all this madness. We, the created beings, have forsaken God the Creator. Man feels he can live by his own rules. The result will simply lead to more havoc everywhere.

Many who labored hard to secure for themselves and their families a piece of the American dream now see their dreams eroded through violent encounters with those who show no regard for others. Covetousness, forbidden by the Ten Commandments, feeds the waters of theft and robbery among the citizens. The constant quest to attain the latest fashion, cars, etc., continues to open wide the gullies of criminal activity in America and elsewhere. This selfishness is forcing the waters of wickedness to breach the levees of civility and godliness that once held society in check.

Drugs, like surging river torrents, have seized the country's neighborhoods. Drivers must close the windows of their automobile to block the pungent smell of marijuana wafting from the car ahead of you on the road! It's unthinkable that your neighbor's house next door could be a meth lab. How far from shore have we drifted? Too far!

On Wednesday, April 24, 2019, President and First lady Trump arrived via Air Force One in Atlanta where he addressed the 2019 Drug Abuse Summit at the Hyatt Regency Hotel downtown. In his address, the President vowed not to stop until America's opioid crisis has ended. Prescription drug addiction has taken its toll on too many victims. President Trump announced that he is trying to criminalize the distribution of fentanyl from China to the United States. This, he believes, will decrease fentanyl overdoses drastically.

In its article titled "The Opioid Crisis", the American Society for the Positive Care of Children (SPCC) stated that 115 people in the US die daily from opioid overdose. The abuse of prescription pain relievers, heroin, and fentanyl has become a national tragedy. The number of pregnant women using opioid pain medicines has grown tremendously in the past few years. As a result, many babies are born with a condition called Neonatal Abstinence Syndrome (NAS).

The article goes on to state that eighty percent of the world's supply of opioid pain medication is consumed by Americans. Yes, the water is rising and we're in the deep end of the pool!

In a newspaper article by Jerry Redmon (Atlanta Journal-Constitution, June 1, 2019, section A10), he states that visits to the emergency room and hospitalizations for overdoses related to opioid use rose 14% from 2017 to 2018 in Georgia. This was based on early info provided by the Georgia Department of Public Health.

The Bible lets us know that no matter how many police officers are hired, they watch but in vain! (Psalms 127:1). I applaud our policemen for the services they render. They are to be commended and respected! However, the authorities can't do it all, we must all do our part, too. If we don't repent and amend our ways, we are in the path of an impending tsunami of trouble.

We are bombarded with troubling news accounts of corruption, crime, death, and destruction! Many people just simply stopped watching the news because it's become so disheartening. Too many of our educational, governmental, religious, and sports figures have become entangled in the underbrush of evil lurking beneath a supposedly calm surface.

The leaders of our American government are also our lifeguards as well. Sadly, many of them are dealing with accusations of sexual misconduct, unethical business practices, and political corruption that has led to great distrust of those chosen to lead us. They are part of the undertow that pulls hapless victims farther out to deep waters. When righteous men are in authority, the people rejoice. However, when wicked people are in power, the people mourn (Proverbs 29:2).

As Christians, Apostle Paul (Philippians 2:15) enjoins us to be blameless and harmless, without rebuke in the midst of a crooked and perverse generation. He further reminds us that we are to shine as lights in the world. The lifeguards have been trained to rescue us from danger and to ensure everyone is safe. It's hard to rescue a drowning victim when the rescuer is floundering too. According to the words of Jesus, when the blind lead the blind, they both will fall into the ditch (Matthew 15:14).

Water Rising in High Places

The wicked waters have risen to dangerous levels in high places in our society now. The damaging effects are seen all over the country on such a mind-boggling scale. Never before have we experienced such a rash of sexual misconduct among our leaders as we do now. As stated in the Word of God, that which is done in darkness will come to light (I Corinthians 4:5). Trust in our elected officials, educators, employers, and even our spiritual leaders is eroding. These are the ones who were models of honesty and integrity. Now, these same leaders are allowing us to drift into deep water by their own patterns of depravity, lawlessness, and perverted justice.

In America, even the political tidewaters continue to rise. The White House sat amid murky waters of the Mueller investigation of Russian collusion during the 2016 Presidential campaign. Paul Manafort, President Trump's former campaign chairman allegedly had ties to Russian intelligence, and supposedly shared political polling data. Many felt that this alleged Russian interference may have helped Trump's presidential bid for the White House, ensuring defeat for the Democratic Party.

After much name-calling and political chaos, there was a call for impeachment of President Trump. Opponents alleging that unethical maneuverings of the President and other members of the White House staff was cause for his removal from office. Democrats claimed that the President abused his power and obstructed Congress from investigating charges that he pressured a foreign power to spy on his political rivals. Arguments for and against the president contributed to the flow of American discontent. Finally, on Wednesday, February 5, the Senate squashed an effort by House Democrats to remove President Trump from office when they acquitted him of those charges.

Another divisive issue was President Trump's determination to build a momentous and expensive wall on America's southern border with Mexico, presumably to stem the tide of illegal immigrants flooding to the United States via Mexico. This contentious issue at one time sparked a shutdown of the nation's federal government. As a result, thousands of federal workers were furloughed, with some still working but not knowing when they would be paid. Can you imagine the uncertainty of not knowing when your mortgage and other bills were going to be paid?

In January 2019, President Trump went on national television stating his case for building the wall, requesting around five billion dollars to construct this steel barrier. He vehemently defended his stance, citing criminal elements, including a case where an elderly Georgia man was brutally murdered. He also felt that the wall would help stem the flow of drugs into the U.S.

Building the wall was one of his campaign promises, stating that Mexico would pay for it.

Our president also hinted that he might declare a national emergency, bypassing the House Democrats to secure the funding. In a meeting with the President, the Democrats said "No" to his request, prompting the President to walk out of the meeting.

So here was America, at an impasse with its leader, wondering how to secure our border with Mexico. A steel wall is a partial fix to slow the tide of illegals into the U.S., but it takes more than a wall to stop unauthorized entry into the U.S. The Bible states (Psalms 127:1)

That except the Lord keeps the city, the watchmen's watch is in vain. America's indiscretions and violence has opened a hole in the dam that's not easy to plug. Slowly America succumbs to the rising floodwaters of evil.

As if the pandemic had not already caused enough misery, the Presidential election in November 2020 fueled heated contention between the Republican and Democratic parties in America! President Trump (R) and his supporters alleged that the votes were fraudulent, and that the election was 'stolen' by Joe Biden's supporters, giving the Democratic party the advantage. President Trump's incessant tweets stirred up waves of discontent across America! Election workers manning ballots at polling sites were placed on observation to insure proper counting of ballots. Still, the allegations of fraud continued, even from President Trump himself!

Cast into waters already boiling with rage, was the Senate race in Georgia. Democrats Jon Ossoff and Raphael Warnock ousted Republican incumbents David Perdue and Kelly Loeffler. By winning these seats, the Democrats gained the majority in the U.S. Senate. Trump also lost the presidential race in Georgia. The country was shocked to see Georgia turn from a red (Republican) to a blue (Democrat) state. This did not sit well with many, especially President Trump!

With the elections over and the Republicans defeated at the polls, protesters voiced their resentment at rallies held around the country. The American voters had elected a Democrat, Joseph R. Biden, Jr. as the 46th president of the United States. Mr. Biden had served as Vice-President from 2009 to 2017 under President Barack Obama. He also was Delaware's senator from 1973 to 2009.

The newly elected Vice-president of the United States is Kamala D. Harris. She stands out as America's first female Vice-President and the first woman of color to hold the second highest office in the U.S. She served as a senator from California and District Attorney for San Francisco.

Gradually the nation began to accept the changing of the guard despite repeated allegations that the election was 'stolen'. Even after recounts of votes in key states like Arizona, Pennsylvania, and Georgia, it was verified that the counts were accurate. Incumbent President Trump had lost his bid for four more years in the Oval Office! It would not be, however, as smooth a transition of power as usual. The nation began planning for Inauguration Day in January 2020.

On January 6, 2021, Congress convened at the Capitol to certify Biden's election victory. Meanwhile, back at the White House, many of President Trump's supporters had gathered to protest election results. The President encouraged them to take their protest to the Capitol. Though barricades were in place around the Capitol building, the protesters pushed past them while clashing with police. The protesters then stormed the Capitol, breaking windows as they rushed inside. Our nation's capital was under siege! The scene was a chaotic one! One person was shot dead by police. Hundreds of Trump supporters invaded the Capitol, interrupting the vote-certifying process. The world watched in disbelief as this drama was televised! What we saw was violent insurrection normally seen in other countries. When the melee was over, at least four people were dead and damage was quite extensive! Take note that this violence was not caused by outsiders, but by American citizens! Later, despite the earlier upheaval, Congress finally certified Joe Biden as America's 46th president.

While America welcomed a new President and administration, much work lay ahead. Again, one of the country's most pressing needs was to slow the spread of COVID-19 and get people back to work. The economy was still very sluggish in January 2021 when President Joe Biden assumed office. Getting relief to the suffering American people was a priority for President Biden. After much debate, another round of stimulus payments was approved by Congress to help financially struggling families.

While President Donald Trump grappled with ways to alleviate COVID-19 and revive the economy, our country dealt with another divisive issue. As a result of his alleged incitement of the Capitol insurrection, many people called for impeachment proceedings. Since Mr. Trump would no longer be in office after January 20, Congress voted to acquit him. President Biden could then focus on the economy and the pandemic.

In Matthew's gospel (Matthew 15: 14), Jesus when describing the sect of Pharisees, said "if the blind lead the blind, both shall fall into the ditch". How can this generation do right when it sees so many leaders in various disciplines doing wrong themselves? Politicians use their power and wealth to hide behind their sexual exploits. Even political races now are tainted by smear campaigns. Teachers seduce the very students they're hired to help develop good character. Trusted clergymen abuse their high office by giving in to lust instead of focusing on cultivating good character that is based on biblical principles. The water is rising, and the shore appears to be getting more distant.

Nature Responds

Aren't we all appalled at the worldwide devastation done by hurricanes, tornadoes, floods, tsunamis, fires, and other natural disasters? The Bible even states that 'the whole creation groans and travails in pain until now' (Romans 8:22). God has been trying to get America's attention, but it seems we're too busy to listen. The book of Proverbs (1: 24-33) God tells us what is happening. He states that God calls us, but we refuse to answer; He has stretched out his hand, but no one pays attention; we disdain His counsel, and want none of his rebuke. So, He says that when our troubles come He will laugh and mock us. Then He says we will call Him, but He won't answer because the people hate knowledge, and choose to not fear Him! Much of the destruction we see is not just coincidences but is a result of the bad choices we make in not pleasing God with the way we live. There is help, but the question is 'do we want it?'

High Water Rising

Yes, we are to help others when calamities occur. That's what civilized people do, rally to the aid of our brothers and sisters in need. All victims are not directly the causes of many of these tragic circumstances, but because we all live in this world together, we too, suffer the effects of evil. To be clear, when people are victims of tragedies, that does not always mean that they are worse than us (read Luke 13: 1-5). As Christ stated in this passage of scripture, 'except we repent, we will perish all likewise'!

Remember the horrific destruction when Hurricane Katrina struck the Gulf Coast in 2005? Such devastation is mind-boggling! The cost in lives lost and property damaged or destroyed is baffling. 2017 was the year of one of the costliest hurricane seasons we've seen in a long time. We recoil at the massive loss of life and property damage of Harvey, which made landfall on August 26, 2017. Texas and Louisiana bore the brunt of this storm. Irma, a few weeks later in September, tore through Florida and the Carolinas. Around September twentieth, Maria devastated the island of Puerto Rico. We remember the warnings issued in various localities in the path of these storms. The water is rising! Residents were ordered to evacuate. Some chose to ride out the storms while most people heeded the warnings. Some stayed and suffered loss of life or injury. Just as the flood waters were devastating then, so are the flood waters of evil sweeping this country now. The water is rising! The currents are swift and deadly!

Monday, January 15, 2018, Dr. Bernice A. King, youngest daughter of Dr. Martin Luther King, Jr. and Coretta Scott King, was the keynote speaker at the 50th Annual MLK Jr. Commemorative Service. In her address to the crowd at historic Ebenezer Baptist Church, she reminded the audience that because of the prevailing bigotry and hatred among us, even all creation is groaning in travail. It is with expectation that we all await the day when all people can live in this one world, with one Father, and in peace. We must realize that name-calling and other forms of disrespect only fuel the fires of hatred that eventually leads to other evil acts.

We prayed for the victims of the raging wildfires in California. The reports of fires breaking out seemed to never end! Think of all the real estate destroyed, manpower exhausted to contain the fires, and even the damage done to the land itself. Groundcovers decimated by the fires lead to other problems. Now flooding and mudslides contribute to the misery of an already bad situation. Many structures are lost, the landscape changed, and even more people perished. Were these just incidents, or have waters of wickedness risen so high, and we don't see them.

May 3, 2018, saw the eruption of Kilauea Volcano in Hawaii, with that state being placed on high alert. Orders for mandatory evacuations were issued on the Big Island. The towering plumes of volcanic ash, along with the molten lava oozing from numerous fissures, destroyed everything in its path. The widespread destruction resembled scenes out of a horror movie! I wondered to myself if this could be a preview of what Hell must be like.

Meanwhile, in August 2018, firefighters in California worked feverishly battling the gigantic blaze allegedly started by an arsonist. Known as the Holy Fire, this fire began in the Holy Jim Canyon area of Orange County. More than 20,000 acres were burned. This was just one of several wildfires raging across California during the summer of 2018.

The widespread destruction resembled scenes out of a horror movie! I wondered to myself if this could be a preview of what Hell must be like!

Meanwhile, in august 2018, firefighters in California worked feverishly battling the gigantic blaze allegedly started by an arsonist. Known as the Holy Fire, this fire began in the Holy Jim canyon area of Orange County. More than 20,000 acres were burned. This was just one of several wildfires raging across California during the summer of 2018.

In November of 2018 as well, another devastating fire raged relentlessly in California. More than 80 people lost their lives in the Camp fire in northern California. More than 12,000 structures were destroyed in this fire. Particularly hard hit was the city of Paradise, which was virtually destroyed. To the south, the Woolsey Fire along Woolsey Canyon Road in Los Angeles County, ignited November 8, 2018. Nearly 1500 buildings were burned, and three persons died.

Malibu, home to movie stars and entertainers suffered extensive damage as homes near the Pacific Coast Highway were reduced to smoldering rubble.

May 2019 will go down in history as having more tornadoes on record than any other May in the USA. According to the National Weather Service, May is typically the month with the most tornadic activity. This year more than 45o tornadoes had already been reported along with catastrophic flooding across the United States. The losses in terms of lives and property are astounding!

Feeling Winter Fury

With America firmly in the crosshairs of the COVID-19 pandemic, and the economy topsy-turvy, winter unleashed its icy vengeance across the nation in February 2021. Bringing brutal and unusually frigid temperatures, ice, and record snowfall, the South was unprepared for winter storm Uri. Snow fell from Washington state all the way down to New Mexico and Texas. Houston was forced to close its airports due to icy conditions. Tennessee roads were coated with ice, creating havoc for travelers. Massive power outages occurred as first sleet fell, then snow, accompanied by gusty winds.

For the southern U.S., this weather was unprecedented. Cities in Texas saw subzero temps and power outages. Louisiana struggled to cope with the ice and snow. Alabama, Tennessee, Arkansas, and Oklahoma were at the mercy of ole man Winter. To make matters worse, a few days later, the South, already reeling from Uri's crippling effects, was hit by a second winter storm named Viola. This storm also blew over the South, making tis way across the Eastern U.S.   Seeing the chaos and ensuing misery called to mind the words of Apostle Paul (Romans 8:22)

"For we know that the whole creation groans and travails in pain together until now". Nature even suffers now as sin engulfs the world.

Even Nature is distraught by all the wickedness on planet earth! The whole creation travails in pain. So much sin has contaminated the earth that it's almost unbearable!

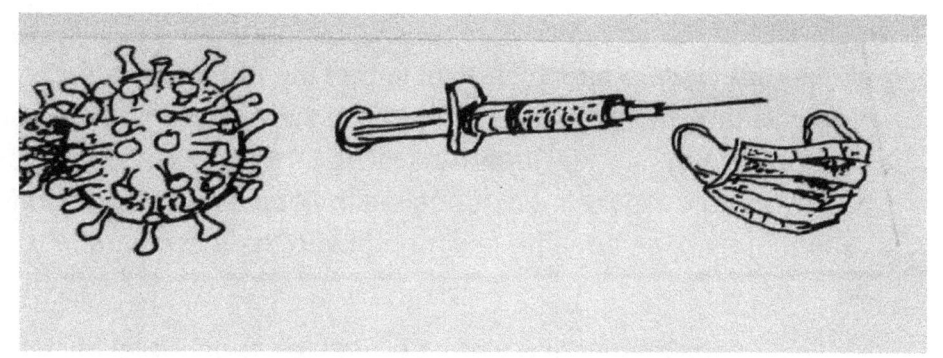

Coronavirus Pandemic of 2020!

The year 2020 will certainly be remembered as a devastating year of global misery! What began as a trickling of the waters in December 2019, soon emerged as a global torrent of sickness and death worldwide by March of 2020. WHO finally called this outbreak a pandemic because of its reach in countries all over the globe. Horrific torrents of misery were unleashed upon the world! The Center for Disease Control and Prevention (CDC) announced an outbreak of another respiratory illness. This coronavirus, COVID-19 for short, is said to have originated in Wuhan, China, affecting thousands in that country. Both the CDC and World Health Organization (WHO) worked feverishly trying to stem the growing tide that became pandemic in scope. Countries worldwide reported alarming cases of the coronavirus. America was not spared as illnesses and death rates spiraled daily. It became unpredictably hard to tell where the next case would occur. Many people who appeared healthy were found to be asymptomatic, meaning that the individual is a carrier of the disease but shows no symptoms. As a result, people were advised to stay six feet apart in public. Hospitals and medical centers were overwhelmed struggling to keep up with demand for treatment as beds became fewer and even the tests were hard to come by.

This brings to mind the word 'pestilence' in the Bible. My hope and trust are in God who says (Psalms 91:3) that the Lord will deliver us from the snare of the fowler and from the noisome pestilence. A pestilence is a fatal epidemic disease. Despite the worldwide reach of this pandemic and the disastrous impact it has made on the world, I still wonder how many of us take note that the water has risen high around us. Is it high enough for us to change our ways? Again, God reminds us in his Word (Proverbs 1:24- 29) that He calls us, and people refuse. He said His hand is stretched out and no man regards it. As a result, we are experiencing trouble such as many of us have never seen before. The reason is also stated that it's because people hate knowledge and do not choose to give God the reverence due Him!

Who would have imagined that the global calamity we see now would occur in our lifetime! The world is in the grips of a seriously catastrophic pandemic! COVID-19 has wrought havoc on such a global scale and is changing life as we know it drastically!

The world's economies suffered tremendously in 2020! Restrictions on airlines and ship cruises affected a lot of people. Some passengers were not allowed to disembark from ships for days, even with sick persons aboard. In the ensuing panic, cleaning supplies and masks disappeared quickly from store shelves. The American stock market dropped over 2000 points in one day. Here at home in America, so many businesses failed and shut down completely. Thousands of employees lost their jobs. Schools and colleges around the world were forced to close. Travel has been reduced significantly. Here at Atlanta's airport, it was strange seeing jets parked along the tarmac, idled because people are afraid to travel! Citizens had been asked to stay at home (referred to as shelter-in place) with some places even placed on curfew. More and more cities asked people to stay home – no jobs, no school, no church, not even being in groups with more than ten people! Curfews were imposed in some places from night until morning! Was God trying to get our attention?

So here we were dealing with the tragedy of the COVID pandemic and its aftermath while still trying to maintain some sense of normal. On one hand, medical experts insisted that if we were to decrease hospitalizations and deaths from COVID-19, we must wear masks, practice social distancing, and limit social gatherings. Many others, however, including city leaders, relaxed mandates requiring wearing of masks in public. Some businesses were given green lights to reopen.

Despite the ravages of the pandemic, increases in crimes continued. Even here in Atlanta, the number of shooting deaths kept rising. The 'city too busy to hate', fell victim to a growing murder rate. As already noted, the waters rise, and we are caught in the relentless currents! My eyes fell upon another Bible passage (Psalm 69:2). David asks God to save him because he was sinking in a deep mire. He felt that he was in an overwhelming flood.

The twenty-third Psalm (Psalm 23:2) declares that because the Lord is his shepherd, David is led beside still waters. Still waters represent peace and quiet refreshment. The world is in turmoil. People are worried about the economy, children's education, health, and life in general.

Deaths of American Personalities

America also lost some outstanding personalities during 2020. Alex Trebek, well-known host of TV game show Jeopardy, and Kobe Bryant, star basketball player for The LA Lakers, both died in January. Civil Rights leader Reverend Joseph Lowery passed in March of 2020. Rock and Roll legend, Little Richard, died in May, while Congressman and Civil Rights icon John Lewis, died in July. In August, we lost Chadwick Boseman, who starred in the movie *Black Panther.* Atlanta Braves baseball Hall of Famer Phil Niekro, along with country singer superstar, Charley Pride, both passed in December 2020. Later in 2021, more of America's famous citizens would also die. Award-winning actress Cicely Tyson left us in January. March 2021 saw the passing of business executive and Civil rights activist Vernon Jordan as well.

Economic Woes

As a result of the severe blow to the economy, our government implemented a plan to give Americans financial help. In the last few months of President Trump's administration, this help came in the form of coronavirus economic impact stimulus checks. These checks sent from the Internal Revenue Service were meant to stimulate the economy. Millions of America's families were able to survive due to the government's intervention.

As the world attempts to fix its ills and not look to God for solutions, we tend to drift further away from peace and calm.

Again, without Jesus, we can do nothing! (John 15:5). Wave after wave of distressing news inundated news channels like a never-ending tsunami. Everyday brought reports of more misery and deaths! Citizens looked like masked robots when one saw them in public! Fear was mirrored on the faces of so many people everywhere you went.

Many of us with loved ones in senior care facilities waited anxiously as we were told we couldn't even visit them for the time being. Keeping a six -foot distance between you and the next person became the order of the day in an effort to stop the spread of the coronavirus which at first seemed to be a virus affecting only the elderly. Later, the virus even spread to younger children as well. In all my days, never had I experienced such paralyzing fear gripping not only America, but the entire world! Everything changed! The world had flipped upside down! The 'new normal usurped its authority over all the world! Even funeral homes changed their ways of conducting memorial services, too. Again, without Jesus, man's efforts are in vain! (John 15:5).

Education of our children was really disrupted as schools shut down. Students had to resort to virtual learning at home. Many parents became frustrated trying to navigate the technology of computers and the internet. The absence of physical interaction with peers and teachers proved to be a great hindrance for some children. These obstacles only caused more stress for families.

I missed the students and staff at school. After retiring from teaching middle school in 2017, I decided to return to the classroom as a Substitute teacher. I felt a sense of purpose in helping our children prepare for the future. Sadly, COVID-19 shut schools down as well. It was in March 2020 that ended the school year.

Faithful church goers also noticed with alarm how the way we worship had been affected by the coronavirus as well. Many churches shut down, choosing rather to live stream or have conference calling or other methods to reach the faithful. Even as I write, I reflect on the last Sunday in-person worship service at our church in East point, Georgia. It was Sunday, March 22, in 2020. Conference-calling, WEBEX, and Facebook Live became the means of churching.

So now every aspect of our society was impacted! Past warnings to seek the Lord fell on a lot of deaf ears. Must we continue to be obstinate and stay on the disastrous path we tread? Is there anyone who sees the pit for which we're headed and wishes to change directions? "Amend your ways and your doings", says the Lord of Hosts (Jeremiah 7:3). Amend means to alter or correct our ways. It's past time to change and return to God!

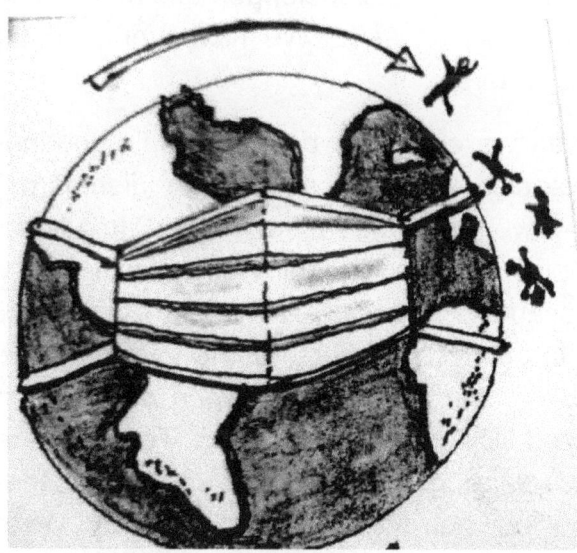

Once more, I'm reminded of the Lord's response to man's haughty transgression of his laws. The Bible passages in Isaiah chapter 24 so clearly paints a picture of the miserable state in which we find ourselves. Verse ten explains the 'shelter-in-place' scenario where every house is shut up, so that no one may come out or go in.

It's time we take a good long look at ourselves. This country evolved partly out of a quest for religious freedom. We were for a while a country grateful to God for his divine blessings that affords us the right to life, liberty, and the pursuit of happiness. With the passing of time, we've become so entrenched in self-gratification that we've lost sight of our original goal. There was a time when God was first in our lives and how we treated our fellow man second. In the race to get our share of the American pie, it's every man for himself. In many homes, God is just an afterthought.

God's plan for mankind centers around love. We are to love God above any other person or anything, and then our neighbors as ourselves. We have sidestepped this most basic principle and turned our focus on self. We have ventured too far out into dangerous waters!

How can we expect to bask in God's goodness and mercy when the society we live in so blatantly disregards His rules that govern how we live and treat each other? In Atlanta, so much evil exists, not just here, but in many other locales as well. I mention Atlanta because I live here. Never did I dream that UPS trucks would be targeted by robbers, just to take packages at gunpoint. A growing number of our young men and women are robbing, stealing, and killing at alarming rates. Too many people now feel it's okay to use drugs. Meth houses dot the landscape, putting the lives of our children and others in jeopardy. Where will it end? What happened to the commandments 'do not kill' and 'do not steal'? Who's bold enough among us to proclaim the truth? Where are the preachers that serve as lifeguards for a world that's floundering in sin's deep waters? Heed the call now before it's too late! The water is rising higher around us as we sleep.

Our moral standards have declined, leading to an increase of cultural depravity in our society. The youth are fascinated with musical lyrics that reduce our women to sexual objects. Sex has become a god in America. As a result, incest, rape, molestations, and homosexuality has surged out of control! Keep in mind that the lifeguard's duty is to warn the people of dangers in the water. Unfortunately, many refuse to heed the warnings until it's too late. Well, people, the water is rising dangerously fast! The whistle is blowing. The lifeguard frantically waves his hands yelling "Get out of the water now"!

The increase in frequencies of sexual molestation and rape is another indicator of the shameful pollution that has seeped into society's reservoir. It is indeed unsettling how we've allowed the bedrock of civility and respect to become so eroded. How long will this erosion of humanity's basic values continue? Modern man has set aside God's laws with ideals of our own.

What we see happening is the scriptures being fulfilled. Apostle Paul's epistle to Timothy

(2 Tim. 3:1) describes these times as the "last days". These perilous days identify Man as covetous, blasphemers, boasters, unthankful, disobedient to parents, and lovers of pleasure more than lovers of God.

Our women and children have fallen prey to the sadistic and selfish desires of those whose sense of decency and godliness seems to have washed out to sea! What has happened to us? The devil has cast his net of evil spirits on humanity. God has provided us with the sandbags that we need to hold back the floodwaters that threaten to drown us in depravity. He can only really rescue us now. He throws us a lifeline. It's up to us to grab it and be pulled to safety. The waters continue to rise, and the currents are too strong for us to go it alone. We need God's help!

One has simply to listen to the evening news to hear that now our females can hardly venture outside and feel safe. How did society sink so low in our morals? No one is safe from sexual predators now. It doesn't matter whether one is an infant or a grandmother. This is a wicked disgrace and shame upon our character. For a country founded on godly principles, we've really deviated from such ideals a lot!

It's unthinkable what our children must endure on their treacherous journeys in life! The headlines and newscasts reek of waters of evil everywhere. From classroom teachers, sports coaches, clergymen, politicians, and even parents, a swirling cesspool of filth has contaminated the lives of the innocents! As a result, we're raising a generation of angry and confused youth.

They didn't get this way by themselves!

As a retired teacher-turned-pastor, it is quite disheartening to see the built-up anger in the children who are subjected to such outrageous violence. Then we wonder why the shootings and other disruptions occur in our communities. We are charged by God to be the protectors of our children and nurture them. We are to be their reservoir of peace, love, joy, and security. Instead, we've become purveyors of sin. The runoff from the cesspools of evil in our community has so contaminated us that everybody is suspicious of his neighbor. Trust is a thing of the past in large part. People steal, kill, rob, and destroy with little or no remorse at all!

One morning while sitting on my patio, a scripture came to mind. Apostle Paul exhorts the people on the Day of Pentecost to "save themselves from this untoward generation" (Acts 2:40). I visualize humanity treading water. Instead of trying to head back to the safety of the shore, we slowly slip into deeper water. We need to take a real look around us and see that the water level (evil) is rising higher. This generation slips farther and farther away from God! It is up to each of us to heed the warnings or risk being pulled under by the evil currents prevailing in society.

Out of Control

All the foundations of the earth are out of course (Psalms 82:5). When we look at our institutions of learning, politics, religion, finances, etc., things are out of control. All of the federal funding to various programs to help schools and develop new policies to make life better and safer, seem to fail. You cannot legislate these issues away. They require more than a band aid. When a nation walks away from God, serious consequences follow. To reverse the current and be able to get back to shore, America must REPENT! Until then, 'evil men will get worse and worse' (2 Timothy 3:13). Notice the increase in shootings across our country! Home invasions, robberies, kidnappings, sexual immorality in the communities and by political leaders, are signs that we are drowning, gasping for air to survive! We must turn back, or the current will carry us far out to sea.

Even though Apostle Paul wrote to church people in Rome (Romans 3:12-18), the description of people's behavior in his day mirrors today's world. He enumerated evils that permeate our society today – people full of cursing and bitterness, murderers, destructive, miserable, with little peace – and the reason is that in general we have lost the fear of God! The Apostle Peter, when preaching on the Day of Pentecost, encouraged the multitude of people listening to "save themselves from this untoward generation" (Acts 2:40).

Today's culture centers on self-pleasure more than God. As a result, the world is rocked by violence, corruption, hatred, and general disregard for human civility. Humanity is trying to survive devoid of God's guidance. Jesus reminds us (John 15:5) that without Him we can do nothing. Outside of God, our world is doomed for failure!

America is experiencing horrific tragedies that involve gun violence. Some cry out for tougher gun control laws, stricter background checks, and restricting certain types of guns. A lot of debate has occurred discussing measures to reduce these types of crimes. Unfortunately, few people will admit that the core of our problem is the sinful state of heart. We look for things to change for the better, but the scriptures tell us that 'evil men will get worse and worse' (2 Timothy 3:13). In the book of Acts (2:40), the Apostle Peter admonishes us to 'save ourselves from this untoward generation'. Today's generation is exhibiting such unthinkable and most unchristian-like behavior! According to Luke (21:26), people are suffering heart failure due to fear of the things that are happening around us.

In March of 2021, Atlanta, Georgia experienced an alarming rise in crime, especially shootings. On March 16, a 21-year-old man took the lives of eight people at three metro Atlanta spas.

Many wondered if the killings were racially motivated as six of the victims were Asians. The city was stunned by such senseless violence. Allegedly the suspect was apprehended by authorities about 150 miles away from Atlanta. Reportedly, he was on his way to Florida to continue his rampage!

Meanwhile, in Colorado, on March 22, another young man killed ten people, including a police officer, at a grocery store there. Just days after the Colorado mass shooting, Atlanta police arrested another young man who entered a Publix supermarket in Atlantic Station. He was carrying five guns and had body armor. Fortunately, he was apprehended before using the weapons. A mass shooting also took place at a FedEx facility in Indianapolis in April. This kind of violence is escalating in different cities across America. Is this a sign of the times now? What has happened to us? The Bible states that evil men would get worse (2 Tim. 3:13).

It seems that the unprecedented disruption of the way of life as we knew it due to the pandemic would have changed our penchant for doing evil! For some this was cause to reevaluate our moral principles and change our behaviors. It was a wake-up call to return to Christian values and respect for God. Unfortunately, not everyone heeds the call! Sin has become a comfortable way of life for far too many people! God is not pleased with many of our ways. God is angry with the wicked every day! (Psalm 7:11).

As we read in the book of Matthew (24: 37 – 39), the Bible states that just as it occurred in Noah's day, so will also the coming of Christ be. People then were living it up, 'eating and drinking, marrying and divorcing, until the day that Noah entered into the Ark'. They did not know what was happening until the floodwaters came and took them away. This is how it will be when Jesus returns for the Church (saved Christians).

Marriage is a sacred institution that was ordained by God (Matthew 19: 4 – 6). Now people marry today and divorce tomorrow. God created male and female to be joined together in marriage. They were to be fruitful and bear children. Fleshly lust is destroying the basic fabric of society, which is the family. As a teacher, I sensed the anger and hopelessness in students because they could not understand why mom and dad were no longer together. The frustration is evident as children express their anguish through acting out in our schools and communities. They join gangs and terrorize neighborhoods. They destroy property and take the lives of others. All this results from disobeying God's laws.

It appears that people are removing all boundaries now, allowing them to feel it's okay to do all kinds of sinful things. The eye of the Lord is looking at all of this! (Proverbs 15:3). No one can hide from God! Do we really believe there is a God who sees what we do? Do we no longer care? It is unbelief that allows people to do the vile and ungodly things they do. The Bible tells us (Psalm 14:1) that the fool says there is no God.

I know that much of what I've written offends some. The problem is that we've tolerated wickedness so long that it's become a way of life and too many of us are okay with that. Colossians (3:5 – 8) informs us that there are certain things that are unlike God that we do that causes 'the wrath of God on the children of disobedience'. Fornication (sexual intercourse between unmarried persons), covetousness (wanting something that belongs to others), filthy communication out of our mouths, to name a few. We hear people constantly walking down the street using explicit language and profanity with no shame! The little kids hear it and it becomes a part of their vocabulary, too. Today's youth are enamored with songs and videos that degrade women and others. Rappers and other singers may live lavishly on the money they make producing such hits, but they do so at the expense of destroying decent and respectable character!

Political leaders, both local and on the national and world level, have stooped to such low levels of conduct unheard of before. Political aspiration is founded on mudslinging, name-calling, and disrespect for civility. Bribery and other unethical tactics pervade the governmental arena. The word of God (Jeremiah 17:11) says a person who obtains riches and not the right way, shall leave them in the midst of his years, and be a fool in the end.

War and Rumors

We live in very volatile times now. Unrest is all around us, here at home as well as abroad. The threat of war is real. The world waits on edge to see where terrorists will strike next. For a while terrorism was something Americans saw happen in other countries. Now such acts of violence are happening on our own soil. They are closer to home and increasing in number. I told you the water is rising!

Warnings about these end time events (Mark 13:7 – 8) let us know that we are in the days of sorrows. Weapons of mass destruction concern our President and military leaders. The verbal threats and warnings keep our country on edge. Now Americans fear the growing threat of nuclear confrontation with North Korea. The verbal tirades between our President Donald Trump and North Korean leader Kim Jong-un seem to push our countries to the brink of war. North Korea has repeatedly launched missiles, testing their military might. Reportedly, one of their latest intercontinental ballistic missiles can reach the US mainland.

In response to the killing of two Americans, Kayla Mueller, American humanitarian worker in Syria, and Army Staff Sergeant Christopher Hake, President Trump directed U.S. Special Forces, to forces, to strike back at ISIS. Abu al-Baghdadi, leader of the Islamic State, was killed in the nighttime raid.

In January 2020, the New Year began with a hint of ominous floodwaters threatening to possibly propel the U. S. into war in the Middle East. President Trump gave orders for a preemptive strike against Qasem Soleimani, leader of Iran's Revolutionary Guards. Qasem was responsible for the death of Sergeant Christopher Hake. The January 2 strike took Soleimani's life, ending his reign of terror. This led to heightened security in America because of concerns for Iranian retaliation

The Middle East has long been a hotbed of tensions. The brutal killing and maiming of hundreds of innocent people for the sake of power is mind boggling! The constant threat of missile attacks, nuclear war, and other atrocities keeps the world in unrest. God is the God of peace, but peace seems to be elusive. When we refuse to accept the Prince of Peace, then the alternative is confusion and unrest.

In May 0f 2021, the Middle East erupted in a cauldron of fighting over the eviction of Palestinian families in East Jerusalem. After clashes between police and protesters at one of Islam's holy sites, al-Aqsa mosque, Hamas unleashed a barrage of rockets into Israel. Israel responded with airstrikes, setting the stage for deadly assaults from both sides.

The skies were lit up at night as Israel's Iron Dome anti-missile system sought to repel rockets launched from the Gaza Strip. Because Gaza is densely populated, many civilian casualties occurred from shelling and airstrikes. Sadly, many of the dead included children.

Reportedly Hamas regularly used residential buildings as bases of their operations. Therefore, Israel destroyed many buildings allegedly used to cover Hamas military assets.

Fear and anxiety practically paralyzed the Gaza Strip region! There were few places for residents to seek cover. With Hamas positioning themselves near civilian living quarters, residents constantly feared becoming victims of Israeli airstrikes.

Israel is a small country when compared to other countries around it. Yet, in spite of its size, God has a special relationship with the Jewish nation. God promised Abraham that his seed would be multiplied immensely and would "possess the gate of his enemies" (Gen. 22: 16-18), (Gen. 24:60). Also take note that God promised Abraham that his name would be great (Gen. 12: 2-3) and he'd father a great nation. God further promised to bless people who blesses Abram. It is through Abram's lineage that "all of the nations of the earth are to be blessed".

Since Israel's birth as a nation in 1948, repeated attempts have been made to destroy this country. It seems that Israel, though embattled, is here to stay because of God's covenant with them. It is especially important to note the prophecy concerning Israel's final victory as foretold in the Bible (Zechariah chapter 14). Jerusalem will be attacked by multiple nations and the city will be taken. But then, according to the text, the Lord will appear and fight against those enemy nations as He stands upon the Mount of Olives.

On Sunday, June 13, 2021, Israel's governing body, the Knesset, approved a new Prime Minister, Naftali Bennett. Prime Minister Bennett was elected to replace outgoing leader

Benjamin Netanyahu whose term spanned a 12-year period. This transition of power followed weeks of fighting between Hamas and Israel.

Here at home, police departments in every city work hard to anticipate and curb outbreaks of violence. Never did we have to be so wary when going to places like the bank, gas station, stores, or even in our own homes. Blood is flowing everywhere and there seems to be no end in sight! Shootings have become the way of life in some areas of our cities. Too much blood is being shed! What happened to "thou shall not kill"? Murders are happening so fast that before you can barely hear the details of one, another has been committed!

Besides the wars occurring in other countries around the world, we are fighting so many wars right here at home. Law-abiding citizens battle for survival against the criminal elements in our communities. Clashes with racist groups mar the peace in cities. Gangs fight each other, leaving trails of fear and death. There is a constant fight for justice for our citizens. The battle between good and evil rages on! Get to safety! The water is rising, America!!

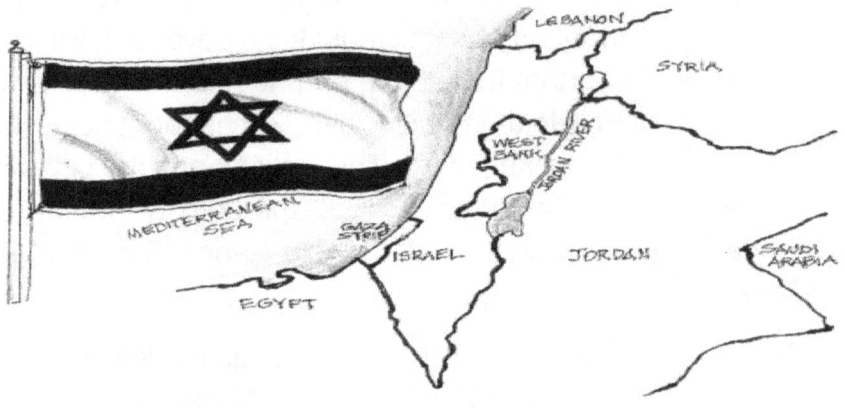

Prosperity - False Security

In December 2020, the world was ready to close the books on the unpleasant memories of the past year. Our hopes rose in anticipation that the new year would bring relief to a world ravaged by COVID-19. We were anxious to return to work, school, and church! Our economy needed a huge boost. Our nerves had been frayed to their breaking point! Things had to get better! High unemployment numbers threatened our economy. Rent and mortgages went unpaid. Food lines stretched for blocks! Many businesses shut down permanently.

Any notions of a quick return to normal were short-lived as we witnessed a steady rise in COVID deaths and hospitalizations. Near the end of January 2021, the number of deaths from the virus reached a staggering 400,000 in America alone! Coupled with the bitterness of racism, high unemployment rates, and rampant crime, the turbulent waters created an ocean of misery everywhere!

Discontent and distrust between law enforcement and people of color certainly contributed to the caustic atmosphere in America in 2020 and continued into 2021. Incidents involving officer shootings of black men forced the issue of racial inequality to the forefront of news in America! National protests erupted in cities across America as angry citizens took to the streets citing police brutality. Curfews were enacted to curb the ensuing violence and mayhem. This was a sad time in our country. We became the talk of the world! African- Americans feared for their lives. Even though there are many good and upright lawmen, the recurring deaths of blacks at the hands of white policemen tainted our perception of lawmen in general.

On March 29, Adam Toledo, a 13-year-old Latino youth, was shot to death by police in Chicago. In North Carolina, on April 21, Andrew Brown was killed by sheriff deputies. This rash of minority killings only heightened distrust and fear in our communities. The economy was in shambles, the pandemic had the world on edge, and social unrest prevailed.

On April 20, 2021, former Minneapolis policemen Derek Chauvin was found guilty in the May 2020 murder of George Floyd. This unnerving act, televised around the globe, resulted in Officer Chauvin's conviction on three counts, based on aggravating factors. Officer Chauvin's knee was on George Floyd's neck for around nine minutes, even though Mr. Floyd was on the ground in handcuffs.

On June 17, 2021, President Joe Biden signed a bill into law recognizing Juneteenth a federal holiday in America. Juneteenth National Independence Day celebrates the end of slavery in the United States. On June 19, 1865, Gordon Granger, a Major General in the Union, announced the end of slavery in Galveston, Texas. President Lincoln signed the Emancipation Proclamation in 1862 and the Civil War ended in 1865. Still slavery continued for a while in Texas. After realizing they were free, blacks began celebrating their freedom yearly on June 19. It was called 'Juneteenth' from then on.

What shall it profit a man if he shall gain the whole world, and still lose his soul? (Mark 8: 36). What is so important that a person will exchange his soul for it? Fame? Friends? Yet this is what has become a priority now for our society. Capitalism has good points but our insatiable appetite for more and has soured the dreams for many. By this I mean so much emphasis is on 'having material things' in order for us to be 'somebody'. As a result, people resort to theft, robbery, home invasions, car-jacking, and other evil means to get what they want. Students are bullied in school because of the clothing and shoes they wear.

Today's culture prioritizes popularity and prosperity. We have lost our focus on what's important in life. When the founding fathers wrote of the 'pursuit of happiness', I don't think they meant for it to come at another person's expense! God wants 'quality and not quantity' from us. Some people feel that if they've accumulated a lot, that God is pleased. The scriptures say that such people think that 'great gain is godliness'. (1 Timothy 6:5).

I thought that by now after experiencing COVID and its aftermath that people would change. God is merciful and wants to bless us, but he also wants us to change our evil ways. It is sickening to see homes burglarized, innocent persons, especially the elderly, cheated out of their savings, and things we've worked hard for taken away by force. Home invasions have become more frequent. The elderly has become prey for wicked people. Sexual depravity is on the rise across all spectrums of society. Opioids and other drug use is wreaking havoc on our youth. This is what happens when a nation forgets who the Creator is. It takes more than money to obtain true peace and happiness. In the book of John (15:5), Jesus states that "without me you can do nothing".

Crime is still a big problem and is getting bigger! Despite efforts by our leaders and lawmen, crime is spiraling out of control. It takes more than an army of police to keep cities safe! In May 2021, Atlanta's Mayor Keisha L. Bottoms announced that she would not seek a second term. Despite her visibility and constant efforts to keep Atlanta "a city too busy to hate", Mayor Bottoms was criticized for the surge in crime during her term. The water is still rising! As we attempt to fix one breach in the dam, another opens up and the evil waters gush out.

It takes more than the mayor, governor, president, and police departments to stem the tide of evil that washes over us. Every individual must look at himself or herself first. Am I a peacemaker or a peacebreaker? Am I living my life according to God's standards? It takes the whole community working together to make this right. "Except the Lord keeps the city, the watchman wakes, but in vain". When God is left out of the equation, efforts to maintain peace and safety are in vain!

In May, Colonial Pipeline, a company based in Alpharetta, Georgia, was targeted by cyber criminals. Fuel shortages occurred in Georgia and states along the U.S. East Coast. Panic caused long lines at gas stations. How quickly things we take for granted every day can change!

Friends, we really are in serious trouble! The Bible (2 Timothy 3:1– 5) refers to today as "perilous times". The Word of God describes this culture as people loving themselves, disobedient to parents, unthankful, unholy, and lovers of pleasure more than lovers of God, just to name a few. As I stated earlier, America, the water around us is rising. Sadly, it seems that we're not aware that we've begun to lose our footing as the sands of time shift beneath our feet.

Danger:deep water!
Turn around! Don't drown!

Some time ago, my wife and I visited Half Moon Cay in the Bahamas. While relaxing in our chairs on the crowded beach, a lifeguard suddenly ran past us. He was blowing a whistle and carrying a flotation device. All heads turned to see why the lifeguard was in such a hurry. Off in the distance, I could see a couple in the water, in an area that was beyond the ropes that defined the safety zone for swimmers. Upon further observation, I noticed that the water the couple were in was the travel lane used by the tender boats that ferried passengers to and from the ship anchored offshore.

After the lifeguard got the couple out of the water, I reflected on the role of a lifeguard.

As the rest of the people frolicked in the water or rested on the beach, the watchful eyes of the lifeguard peered over the crowd, looking for possible dangers. Even though there were lots of people around, it took the watchful eyes of the lifeguard to detect danger. This is what he was hired to do. Earlier, I stated that preachers were like lifeguards. Our job is to watch for the souls of people and warn them in times of danger. Those times are now! The Apostle Paul warned his young protégé Timothy (2 Timothy 3:1) that in 'the last days perilous times shall come'.

If this country doesn't change its course, we're doomed. I pray for America. I pray for our leaders, and leaders around the world. People are worried about the future – finances, education, government, and our spirituality. Fearfulness is beginning to take hold, all because we have turned away from the safe harbor, i.e., Jesus Christ! We see the warning signs all around us daily. What are we doing about it? We wish for peace and safety. In the words of the Apostle Peter (Acts 2:40), we are admonished to 'save ourselves' from this untoward generation. I can't say it enough, 'the water is rising!'

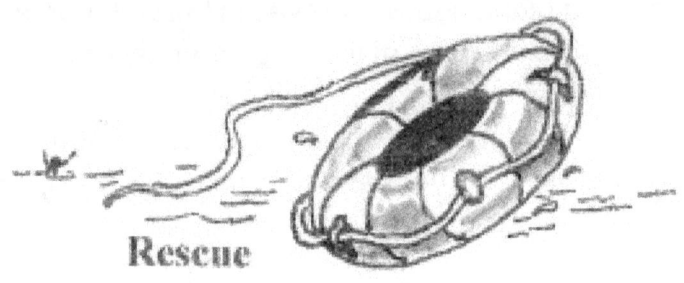

Rescue

The tsunami of troubles sweeping the land with increasing frequency should serve as our' 'wake-up' call. If anyone should heed tho warning signs, it should be the Christians! We must no longer be complacent in our walk with God. It is easy to seek friendship with the world first and make our relationship with God secondary in our lives. In doing so, we relinquish the power and benefits reserved for true followers of Christ. We then succumb to the values of the world system which in general is contrary to the principles of God.

Tap water is good for many uses. When I want coffee, I like it hot, not lukewarm! God wants us to decide whether we're going to be hot, lukewarm, or just cold. We are to choose today whom we will serve, Him or the devil. Whose side are we on? To be a Christian means to stand for all that's right and true according to God's laws. Too many church goers straddle the fence. We go to church on Sunday, but live different lifestyles for the rest of the week! This double standard makes it hard for those outside of Christ to even want to hear about church.

God wants to be our source of joy, peace, and prosperity. He says that if those of us who identify with Him would humble ourselves, pray, turn from our evil ways and seek Him, He would heal our land and bless us (2 Chronicles 7:14). When America resumes our pursuit of God and His righteous ways, our nation will truly become great again! Crime rates would fall, schools would become halls of learning again, respect for life and dignity will once again define the character of our citizens. Blessed is the nation whose God is the Lord! Let's repent and turn the tide for the better.

John 3:16 is a well-known Bible verse that lets us know that God loves us so much that He gave us His only begotten Son (Jesus), so that whosoever believes on Him will not perish, have everlasting life! Do you have that life or are you just existing?

Where Do We Go from Here?

We must ask ourselves "Where do we go from here?" As late as August 2021, the economy still struggles to rebound, crime seems to be on the uptick, and the new surge of COVID-19 reminds us that we're not out of the woods yet. Remember that God calls us to do right, but when we refuse to hear Him, He will not ANSWER us when we call Him. (Proverbs 1:24-29).

If people would just pause for a moment to think of all the good things that God has done for us, I feel that we'd change our attitudes towards Him. In the book of Romans (Rom. 2:4), Apostle Paul asks his audience if they despise God's goodness, longsuffering, and patience. He further states that the goodness of God should ultimately lead one to repentance.

One Friday morning in February, I eulogized another friend. I pondered what scripture to use in my address to family and friends left behind. I choose a passage from Psalms (Psalms 90:12). The writer asks God to 'teach us to number our days, so that we may apply our hearts to wisdom' . We need the wisdom of God in order to live lives in peace and righteousness. We can't live just any kind of way and expect that when we die everything will be alright with God! The Bible states (Eccl. 11:3) that in the place where a tree falls, that's where it shall be. If I die in sin,

I shall remain in my sins to be judged by God.

As we approach the end of summer 2021, the waters still churn around us! The rumblings of war can be heard as the Taliban, who consider themselves to be Islamic purists, use ruthless tactics to gain control of Afghanistan. The lives of thousands of Afghans and Americans are in

jeopardy. The airport in Kabul is swamped as people try to flee the country and escape the brutality of the Taliban. With the United States committed to withdrawal of its peace-keeping forces by the end of August, the Taliban now have free reign to rule the area.

Meanwhile, back at home, America contends with an upsurge of COVID cases as the Delta variant spreads throughout the nation. This time, many children fall victim to this highly contagious form of the virus. Still, there seems to be no break in the rising scourge of homicides in our communities! Cities like Chicago and Atlanta continue to see an alarming increase in shooting violence that baffles many. What's happening to us? Will our communities ever be safe again?

The prophet Jeremiah (Jeremiah 6: 16-17) urges the people to look around and ask for the 'old paths' and 'good ways' and walk accordingly. The people responded, "we will not". This is the same callous attitude of society today! Despite pleas of God's preachers (lifeguards) to repent and change our ways, people refuse to do right. Hence the water keeps rising around us!

The evil waters rush through our cities causing havoc everywhere. Murders occur more frequently, and sexual crimes are rampant! The Old Testament prophet Amos gives us a hint of the source of our problems. Through Amos (Amos 8; 11-12), God tells the people that there's a famine coming in the land. He explains that it's not a famine of food, but of hearing of the word of the Lord! In other words, the masses of people don't want to hear the truth from God. Despite all the calamities happening in our world, many of us refuse to do what's right! This is madness! We're on a path to destruction.

John 3:16 tells us that God's love for us is so deep that He wants us to have an everlasting life. In order to bask in His love and live the victorious life, we have to change our ways. It's past time to repent of our wrongs and seek God's guidance to stop the massive barrage of evil that floods the land. Let's turn and heed the call to return to the safety of God and not be swept to our deaths by the tsunami of sin! Until we begin to stop the breaches, the water will continue to roar as it rises around us!

It is late in the evening and there is a little light left before the sun sets. We have waded too far out and need to turn and head to shore immediately! The currents are too strong for us to navigate on our own. Jesus is tossing us a lifeline but it's up to us to catch it if we want to be rescued. Why be stubborn and drown? Repent, brothers and sisters, be baptized in the name of Jesus, to remove your sins. Then He will fill us with His spirit (Holy Ghost) so we can be one of His dear children (Acts 2:38-40).

Jesus shed His own blood for you and me. If we die unsaved, it is not because He wills it so, but rather we do so of our own choice. Jesus pleads with us to 'look unto Him, all the ends of the earth, and BE SAVED'. Once more I plead with you, as a 'lifeguard' hired by God, to heed the warning! The water is rising fast!! Let's all REPENT! There's a storm out on the ocean, and it's moving toward us fast!

My fellow Americans, to truly make America great again, we must return to God! We have an adversary, the devil, who like he did in the Garden of Eden, has deceived us. People feel it's okay to do the devious and ungodly things that are being done in our society. People boldly steal, rob, kill, cheat, and destroy property and feel good about it.

The scriptures (1 Peter 5:8) inform us that the devil seeks for someone to devour. If we resist him, he will flee from us (James 4:7). Too many people give in to Satan and are under his control. The heartless murders, kidnappings, sex crimes, to name some, are not of God! This is motivated by the devil.

The devil is characterized as a thief (John 10:10). He comes for no other reason but to steal, kill, and destroy. Jesus is the answer for He came that we might have abundant life. As a nation, we've become so focused on material gain that we've pushed God out of our lives. What shall it profit a man if he gains the whole world and lose his soul? (Mark 8:36).

Blessed is the nation whose God is the Lord (Psalms 33:12). God's face is against them that do evil (Psalm 34:16). So, what do we do to change our course? The answer is to fear God and keep his commandments. This is the duty of man. (Eccl.

12:13). We will try everything else but God to remedy society's ills, but Jesus says that without Him we can do nothing! (John 15:5).

On the Day of Pentecost, after Peter had preached to the crowd in Jerusalem, the bible says they were pricked in their hearts. They realized they were on a collision course and needed to change their ways. The question was asked "what shall we do?" Peter's response (Acts 2:38), was that they needed

to **REPENT AND BE BAPTIZED IN THE NAME OF JESUS FOR THE REMISSION OF SIN!** Those who heard the message realized their living was contradictory to God's laws for man. What's your excuse America? Aren't we fed up with the corruption and evil all around us? Isn't it time to seek God and his righteousness? We're already too far out from the shore and the ground on which we stand is no more than shifting sand. Yet we continue to wade farther away from God!

The water is rising higher and higher! Grab the lifeline today! Help our youth find their way back to the shore. Let there be a revival of good moral values, respect for each other, and most of all, a heightened respect for Almighty God and his standards.

Let's get out of this deep water and **RETURN TO GOD!!!!!** God, our creator, has a message for the entire world. He loves his creation and wants us to be happy and be at peace. He is able to sustain His children in our most trying times! He tells us (Isaiah 45:22) to look unto Him and be saved, ALL the ends of the earth, for HE IS GOD, and there is none else! This is a plea to everybody! It's time to turn back to the shores of righteousness NOW! The water is too deep and the currents too dangerous! Let's get back on solid footing with God now before the raging waters of sin sweep us out to sea and we perish when we should live.

RIGHTEOUSNESS exalts a nation, but **SIN** is a reproach to any people (Proverbs 14:34).

By God's grace we're still alive to see the year 2022 come in. The floodwaters of the past two years have not completely gone away. Rising crime rates are still a primary topic of concern. Mental health issues plague our nation. While COVID-19 appears to slowly be relinquishing its hold on the world, a new stream called omicron bursts forth and the waters still rise.

Folks, life's normal course has changed for us. If we are to get any reprieve, we must amend our ways! Earlier I mentioned the role of the watchmen, i.e., the preachers. As the scriptures tell us (Ezekiel 3:17-21), preachers are held responsible if they do not warn people of impending danger. God is displeased with the violence and utter wickedness in the world that He created!

Sexual immorality, murder, child abuse, corruption, to name a few, violate God's laws. We reap the bitter harvest from the evil that we sow (Gal. 6:7).

Once more, instead of the waters receding, they continue to rise, and we don't seem to be alarmed at all! Come on brothers and sisters, let's fill the holes and cracks in the land so that the evil waters of sinfulness cease. The time to repent and seek God's face is now! We should want to see our children's children grow up. Let's make conscientious decisions to stop the violence, love people, and do what's right. Let's work together to stop the waters from rising any higher! Let's return to God and live! With rising waters posing imminent threats to humanity, we need to know what strategies to implement to avoid more catastrophes. When a dam breaks, torrents of water are released causing dangerous flooding. People and objects downstream are faced with loss of lives and property damaged or destroyed.

High Water Rising

The dam has already cracked. Despite man's exhaustive efforts to fix things, the breaches continue to widen. The more man attempts to solve his own problems, the more the evil waters are unleashed. Our governmental agencies seek to stem the tide of raging tempest with ideas based on

human reasoning. God's thoughts are not our thoughts, neither are the ways of man the ways of God (Isa. 55:8-9). We're trying to fix a broken system with our humanistic approach. The problem is spiritual and requires help that is beyond human logic. Jesus says (John 15:5) that without him we can do nothing.

The water is high and rising, and the currents are swift. If we are to survive, we must look to God. This message is to the world (Isa. 45:22). The thief (Satan) has no other goal but to steal. Kill and destroy (John 10:10), but Jesus gives us life! Look all around us. Every day we hear and see murders, rapes, kidnappings, robberies, etc. The list of wickedness among us grows daily! As a result, we have become distrustful, fearful, miserable, sick, and unhappy. We must fix this. Don't just wait for the government to fix society's ills. It starts with us individually.

It's time to shut off the valves so the water stops gushing. The path to curbing the relentless surge of evil leads to God! It's not God's will for people to die as we do! Our youth die too young.

The number of suicides has increased. Society is sick! Electronic media has captivated our children's minds. Knowledge about God's redeeming grace has diminished in our homes today.

We've become a society too busy for God. So, we opened the floodgates and allowed rampant sin to invade our communities. Now what was once wrong is okay and right is wrong. For the sake of this generation, let's turn back and shut off the valves of unrighteousness, lest we all drown. Jesus extends each of us a lifeline if we're only willing to reach out and grab it. You and I have a chance to be rescued. Let's grab it before it's too late! Let's **REPENT** and go back to God! He's willing to forgive us and heal our land. It's our only hope! Remember, the water is high and **STILL RISING!**

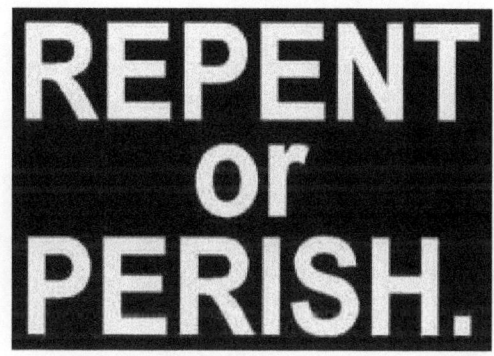

www.ingramcontent.com/pod-product-compliance
Lightning Source LLC
Chambersburg PA
CBHW022118090426

42743CB00008B/903